the PURPOSE *Pivot*

MELISSA GONZALEZ

the PURPOSE Pivot

How Dynamic Leaders Put Vulnerability and Intuition into Action

WILEY

Published by John Wiley & Sons, Inc., Hoboken, New Jersey.
Published simultaneously in Canada.

Library of Congress Cataloging-in-Publication Data

Names: Gonzalez, Melissa author
Title: The purpose pivot : how leaders put vulnerability and intuition into action / Melissa Gonzalez.
Description: Hoboken, New Jersey : Wiley, [2026] | Includes index.
Identifiers: LCCN 2025021886 (print) | LCCN 2025021887 (ebook) | ISBN 9781394329472 cloth | ISBN 9781394329496 adobe pdf | ISBN 9781394329489 epub
Subjects: LCSH: Leadership | Leadership—Psychological aspects | Intuition
Classification: LCC HD57.7 .G6644 2026 (print) | LCC HD57.7 (ebook)
LC record available at https://lccn.loc.gov/2025021886
LC ebook record available at https://lccn.loc.gov/2025021887

COVER DESIGN: PAUL MCCARTHY
COVER IMAGES: © GETTY IMAGES:
(BACKGROUND) COLORS HUNTER—CHASSEUR DE COULEURS
(TAPE) COLORS HUNTER—SKIBA

SKY10126340_091725

This book and journey are dedicated to my dearest loved ones: my daughter and husband, my parents and my in-laws, my siblings, and the chosen family around me I am so fortunate to have. In my best days and scariest ones, you are consistently by my side, and I am forever thankful.

Contents

Preface
Manifestation and the Law of Attraction

Welcome to *The Purpose Pivot*. This book invites readers on an inspiring journey through the real-life experiences of women who have faced challenges that reshaped their perspectives about the relationship between professional success and well-being. By embracing vulnerability and intuition, they have reimagined their purpose and discovered strength and resilience along the way.

At a time when society is craving open dialogue about critical topics—such as the impact of stress on our bodies, the realities of perimenopause and menopause, and the nuances of well-being beyond just wellness—this book seeks to fill that gap. Drawing on dozens of interviews and a year of research, *The Purpose Pivot* serves as both a guide and a companion for women navigating their unique journeys of growth and wisdom.

Whether you are leading in the workplace, at home, or within yourself, my hope is that this book serves as a resource that fuels empowerment through shared stories, experiences, and actionable lessons. You will find over a dozen practical worksheets at the end of this book, in addition to exercises embedded in each chapter, designed to help you apply these lessons to your own life.

The first third of the book establishes a foundation of understanding. From trusting your gut and harnessing the power of intuition, you will learn how your inner voice speaks words of truth—and how to better listen to them. We then break down the science of stress: what it does to your body, how to distinguish positive stressors from negative ones, and how to take back control of your health, both physically and mentally. We also explore how to develop a healthier relationship with the person you see in the mirror every day.

In the middle section of the book, we take a deeper dive into "doing the work." In Chapters 4–8, we explore our Purpose Journey, the process of reprioritization, finding grace in gratitude, the power of community and sisterhood, and the importance of slowing down to reclaim balance. We also address the setbacks that hold us back and learn strategies to navigate them. Finally, in Chapter 9, we bring this exploration full circle by examining the dance between growth and how decluttering and shedding what no longer serves us creates space for purposeful transformation.

This journey begins with my own personal story. And, throughout the book, you will meet numerous inspiring women who have shared their struggles, triumphs, and key learnings. From diverse backgrounds—spanning various ages, professions, and career paths—we will explore topics such as embracing intuition as a leadership tool, aligning our values with our core purpose, and navigating the delicate balance between growth and letting go.

As someone who has spent my professional career analyzing data, trends, and insights to uncover growth opportunities for clients, I turned that same analytical mindset inward. I conducted dozens of interviews, devoured books by enlightening authors, immersed myself in podcasts hosted by leaders in self-help and well-being, and reflected on my own life experience spanning almost five decades. What has been incredible is how this vision has evolved—women introducing me to other women, individuals wanting to be part of this mission of breaking through barriers via shared stories and collective support. The most unexpected yet profound gift has been the opportunity to tell powerful stories of women who trusted me with some of their most intimate experiences.

My Story: The Impetus and Inspiration for This Book

In late 2022, I noticed a marked shift in how I felt day to day. I began experiencing light episodes of vertigo, sluggishness (highly unusual for someone as energetic as I am), and a general sense of being "off." Waking up, once an exciting part of my day, became increasingly difficult.

After attending a women's wellness retreat hosted by Nancy Berger (then chief revenue officer at Hearst), DealMakeHer co-founder Stacy Berns, and *Women's Health* magazine, I realized I needed to prioritize myself. There, I connected with Mona Sharma, a renowned holistic nutritionist, who generously shared her insights. She advised me to get a comprehensive blood panel and recommended dietary changes, such as eliminating salads, reducing dairy, and avoiding gaseous foods.

For months, the lab order sat on my desk, gathering dust. Weeks turned into months, and months into a year. Why? Because I failed to prioritize making the time. And because I also lost sight of the fact that nothing is more premium than personal well-being. While the cost of comprehensive testing—$1,000+—seemed high, I later realized that investing proactively in my health was far more cost-effective than dealing with medical crises. Hindsight is often 20/20.

By fall 2023, my inner voice grew louder, persistently warning me that something was wrong. I spoke about it often with friends and family, suggesting I might need a cleanse or reset. My Raynaud's syndrome flared almost daily, with my extremities turning blue frequently due to restricted blood flow. I had my first bout of shingles, and by December and into 2024 I would go nearly a week at a time without a bowel movement.

After a year of near-constant travel—from Barcelona to Seattle—balancing 14-hour workdays, leadership responsibilities, and being an engaged mother and wife, my body finally gave out. One night, alone in a hotel room across the country from my family, I awoke in excruciating pain, curled into the fetal position on the floor.

It was a wake-up call from the universe to me: *We were warning you.*

Until then, if you followed my social media, you saw a woman thriving—juggling life seamlessly, winning industry awards, jet-setting across the world. And while I loved my career, the gift of travel, the incredible projects, and my speaking engagements, I had been suppressing the warning signs of health.

After I was released from the hospital and able to fly home weeks later, I chose to publicly share my experience. The response was overwhelming. Messages poured in—DMs, texts, emails—from women and men alike, sharing their own struggles and thanking me for my openness. Friends I admired confided in me; one had suffered a stroke but hid it out of shame, now suffering neurological damage from delaying treatment. Others were battling cancer, undergoing radiation, or navigating perimenopause and menopause with little guidance.

In that moment, I knew these conversations needed to happen on a larger scale. We needed to normalize prioritizing self-care within our leadership journeys. Through my recovery, personal exploration, and research, my commitment to well-being deepened. I began getting quarterly blood panels, studying DNA markers, and understanding the complexity of hormones—many of which standard tests overlook. I consulted holistic doctors, nutritionists, acupuncturists, and energy healers, and engaged in deep, one-on-one conversations with women in my network.

While this book does not disclose the names of every contributor due to privacy, it is a culmination of collective learnings. It combines real-world stories from inspirational women with insights from medical doctors, psychologists, nutritionists, and fitness experts. Three high-level recurring themes emerged in my research:

1. The fear of appearing weak by admitting to physical or mental health struggles
2. The belief that we must "power through" until our bodies collapse
3. The immense relief that comes from sharing our journeys and embracing the strength found in vulnerability, and the unexpected gift of our sharing helping others

By joining this journey, you will tap into a growing community that recognizes strength in vulnerability and values exploration as a tool for clarifying purpose. Purpose is our North Star, guiding us through both triumphs and challenges. It helps us redefine our self-perception, our daily habits, and the space we create for what truly matters.

I am deeply grateful for each person who has been part of this journey. Your openness, time, and trust have made this book possible. Together, let's embark on this transformative path—one of growth, shedding, and ultimately, purpose-driven living.

the PURPOSE Pivot

1

Trusting Your Gut

Embracing Intuition as a Leadership Tool

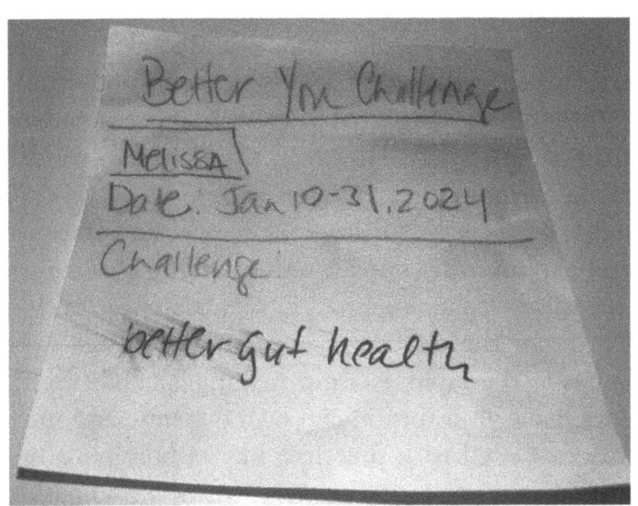

JANUARY 10, 2024, is a date I will always remember.

I was jolted out of my sleep in excruciating pain. Leading up to that time, my inner voice had been telling me "something is not okay," and for the weeks I laid in a hospital bed across the country from my home, I hadn't even remembered the Post-it Note I had written just weeks earlier.

It was a note I wrote with my family on December 25, 2023, as we openly spoke about a "Better You Challenge" we would do together. One person said daily planks, another said she will brush her dogs' teeth daily, another said hydrate more regularly. My note said, "Better Gut Health" and I admittedly wasn't sure how I would accomplish this, but I had planned on a month-long cleanse, starting on January 10, 2024.

Starting that cleanse took on a whole new meaning on January 10, 2024, when I was jolted out of my sleep at three in the morning, rushed to the ER just two hours later, and underwent emergency surgery by 1 p.m. because my intestines had twisted 365 degrees, and I was hours away from going into septic shock.

My woman's intuition had been speaking to me for over a year, and I wasn't fully listening. All I knew was that something was off and what was manifesting inside was getting louder and louder.

Often described as the ability to instinctively understand without conscious reasoning, intuition has long been undervalued, or not fully believed in modern society. However, through real-world narratives and scientific insights, you can see how it serves as a profound force that shapes decisions, fosters resilience, and transforms lives. This chapter explores that impact, interweaving personal stories like mine with studies from psychology, neuroscience, and emotional intelligence. From the duality of cognitive processes explained by William James to the rapid decision-making capabilities highlighted by Malcolm Gladwell, intuition can be a dynamic and indispensable tool to harness. Paired with practices like mindfulness, breathwork, and heightened emotional intelligence, "trusting your gut" can offer a pathway to greater self-awareness, creativity, and purpose in both personal and professional domains. In this chapter we will explore the correlation between trusting your gut and intuition, the role of emotional intelligence, why we often ignore the signs, and how to break those habits.

> **"I need a timeout in life,"** wrote Shirley Ramos Roseman, author of *Thoughts of a Butterfly*, on a piece of paper in 2009, four days before she had a stroke at the age of 29.

When we explore the power of intuition, it can often feel abstract. By studying both time and history, we find numerous demonstrations that intuition exists in a very real way. In Shirley's case her gut and her inner self were speaking to her, not so dissimilarly to how mine was speaking to me. On the outside she was a burgeoning mortgage broker, she was social, thriving, and in her stride, but inside she very much knew something was off and her body was asking her for a break.

Shirley would later learn that she had a hole in her heart and that a blood clot traveled through that hole and made its way to her brain. She'd had a stroke. She was fortunate to be awakened by the tireless ringing of her phone as her mom frantically looked for her when she didn't show up for her brother's party. But Shirley's recovery wasn't seamless, and she needed to evaluate and make life adjustments. While she didn't understand how to decipher what her inner self was whispering to her pre-stroke, what it did open was an awakened spirituality. It opened a closer connection with her thoughts and her actions. It led her to write feverously each day, to slow down, and it taught her to listen more intently to what her mind and body were telling her.

Emotional Intelligence and Intuition

The word "intuition" comes from the Latin *intuir*, which means "knowledge from within." It is often defined as the ability to understand something instinctively, without the need for conscious reasoning. It involves quick judgments based on prior experiences and knowledge.[1,2] The power of intuition is supported by a blended combination of psychological insights, neuroscience, and real-world applications, and our openness to receive and listen to the thoughts that penetrate our minds. It takes not only an awareness but a certain level of emotional intelligence and human cognition to trust the energy.

While it was once shrugged upon and dismissed by scientists, the opportunity of intuition is being embraced more widely today. Through the advent of social media demystifying what intuition means and the sharing of more use cases and examples (some from those as young as three years old), there is a growing openness to the dialogue around the power of intuition. Scientists who study cognitive behaviors have begun to think of intuition *as a set of nonconscious cognitive and affective processes*. While the outcome of these processes is often difficult to articulate and is not based on deliberate thinking, the processes have validity and have been proven to be effective.

If we look at the studies of Malcolm Gladwell,[3] his research suggests that intuitive decisions can be made in seconds, *if we allow it*. And those decisions can be as accurate as analytical ones in certain situations, especially when under pressure, based on one's subconscious processing of information—tapping back on prior experiences, knowledge, and the gut. Through his study and analysis, Gladwell suggests that our brains are capable of synthesizing vast amounts of data rapidly, allowing us to recognize patterns and draw conclusions without conscious deliberation.

Couple Gladwell's studies with the insights of William James,[4] a philosopher and psychologist who was instrumental in establishing Harvard's psychology department in the late 1800s, who believed that cognition takes place in duality—on one end of the spectrum it takes place in an associative manner that is more spontaneous and "effortless," and on the other side it takes place in a rational manner that is analytical with concerted effort and more methodical. He viewed intuition as a way of knowing that bypasses analytical reasoning, allowing individuals to grasp concepts or truths quickly and often without conscious awareness. James also suggested that intuition is informed by past experiences and emotions, enabling people to make judgments based on a holistic perception of a situation. This of course begs larger questions when we see intuition displayed in very young children, but also validates the possibilities of its innate possibilities.

In his work, James also argues that this instinctive knowledge can be as valid as rational thought and recognizes intuition as a powerful cognitive tool that complements rational processes in navigating life's complexities.

However, to embrace intuition, it is not experiences and knowledge alone that enable the action of acting upon it. It also takes the maturation of emotional intelligence. Emotional intelligence (EQ) is linked to the act of intuitive decision-making. People who demonstrate high EQ are often more attuned to their feelings and those of others, enhancing their intuitive capabilities.[5] It has been shown that women tend to be more attuned to our EQ than our male counterparts, as we tend to score higher than men in areas of empathy, interpersonal relationships. and social responsibility.[6] But still we too often dismiss or suppress our intuition capabilities.

Neuroscience of Intuition and Why We Ignore the Signs

In my case, my intuition and my EQ were telling me I was not myself, yet I suppressed both. And if I listened with more acceptance and urgency, I could have been making wiser decisions for my well-being sooner. Why does this happen? Is ignoring the signs more human nature than not?

Scientifically, the right-brain and the left-brain relationship pulls on our tensions of logic and creativity. Studies in neuroscience suggest that intuitive thinking is associated with the brain's ability to process information unconsciously, often utilizing the left hemisphere (logic) more than the right (creativity).[7] In his book *Descartes' Error: Emotion, Reason, and the Human Brain*, Damasio explores the interplay between emotion and cognition in decision-making and the tension between the right and left brain.

It's not a perfect balance, and depending on our natural affinities and tendencies, some of us are more naturally predisposed to logic and some to creativity. Those more heavily weighted in creativity have a more organic openness to exploration and acceptance of the less tangible and therefore embrace new experiences with more comfort. For those who live more in logic, the unknown and the seemingly inexplicable are harder to grasp and accept. When we have more freedom from logic, we are more likely to trust in and react from intuition, or what may feel like more impulse decisions.

Let's put this in practice. Have you had a jittery feeling in the morning but were not sure what you felt so anxious about? Have you ever felt more "off" in your day and instead of pausing to say, "Maybe there is a reason I keep dropping things, or tripping, or missed that train," you ignored the situation? Have you ever had something stop you in your tracks from moving forward but you couldn't understand what was causing such hesitation? Personally, I have felt all those at various points, and more often than not I can trace those feelings to a subsequent "event." Once, while I was shopping for a new pair of shoes, a woman stole my bag, which held my wallet and numerous personal items. Another time, I missed a stabbing I would have otherwise walked in on had I not missed my train. Sounds crazy but both are factual occurrences that happened on the same days I felt all those uneasy feelings and unexplained jitters prior to the actual event.

I consider myself to be a fairly creative spirit, but I definitely have a pragmatic approach. Sometimes creativity and spontaneity win, but from time to time logic leaves me overanalyzing a situation and it pauses my ability to "trust my gut" and embrace my intuition. Sometimes logic paralyzes my ability to decode what my signs of intuition are trying to tell me. Or sometimes I simply deprioritize the importance of listening to what my inner sense is telling me. Nowadays, I try to accept the free flowing more openly and allow it to let me see what I may not otherwise be able to see.

A Look at Mindfulness and Intuition

For Shirley, whom I introduced earlier in this chapter, her near-death experience reacquainted her with her relationship with intuition. In her journey of acceptance and recovery, she began reevaluating life, her connection with nature and with the elements, and became more open to the energy around her. She started journaling daily, worked with a medium as she embarked on her journey to start a family by studying her body and fertility, and found ways to clear out her mental clutter and find a state of presence. In doing this, she found numerous connections between the unconscious mind and true, tangible outcomes and life events.

"We can't always change what's happening around us, but we can change what happens within us."

—Andy Puddicombe, Headspace co-founder[8]

There are a number of ways to embrace mindfulness, and over time those practices will open a deeper relationship with gratitude and ultimately lead to a greater acceptance of the possibilities of an intuitive mind. One avenue toward a mindfulness practice is through our relationship with nature.

Making space for time in nature fires up synapses that we often don't even realize have stopped snapping. (We'll explore this further in Chapter 7.) Whether it's starting by making space to see a sunrise or sunset (my personal favorite), embarking on a walk down a nature trail, or sitting next to a pond and hearing the sounds of running water—finding our space with nature allows in a quietness that simultaneously opens up cognitive space. Mindfulness has also been shown to improve self-insight as well as fear modulation, linked to our brain's middle prefrontal lobe area. A mindfulness practice silences the intense stimulation of daily life and awakens a sense of presence (which we will further explore in Chapter 5) that is often aligned with feelings of gratefulness and fosters an awareness and connection to intuitive thoughts. It also opens our ability to visualize and create thought—what our minds are meant to do.

A Deeper Look at the Power of Breathwork and Mindfulness

As we age, our breaths become shallower and shallower. Muscles involved in breathing, like the diaphragm, can weaken over time, and lung tissue may lose elasticity, leading to narrower airways. *Your lungs mature by the time you are 20–25 years old. After about the age of 35, it is normal for your lung function to decline gradually as you age.*[9]

To celebrate my 40th birthday I took refuge at Miraval Resort, a wellness destination designed to help guests create a life in balance through mindfulness. There I had one of the most cathartic moments I can remember.

One activity involved climbing a ladder that took me four stories in the air, then walking a tight rope that spanned two city blocks. I remember being so exhilarated by the thrill of it that fear was a detached feeling for me. I was wearing my Alo Yoga outfit and my cute sneakers, and had ensured my hair was photo ready! As I climbed to the top of the ladder and looked out across the Sonoran Desert landscape of Tucson, Arizona, all I could take in was the beauty of this triumphant moment, and I was ready to make it across the tightrope. About one-third of the way, my brain began to process what my body was doing:

> "Walking on a tightrope, four stories in the air, with only a cord attaching to a person holding me from the ground."

As that mind-body connection took place, an overwhelming feeling of panic took over my entire being. Not only did I shake from head to toe, but I shook the tight rope so fervently that my coach standing below was in full physical vibration with me. At this point, I was proud of myself that I had gotten even that far. I was fully satisfied with my bravery and yelled down, "I am good, I am going to jump down now." Before I could take the leap, my coach pleaded with me to trust him, to hold off giving up, and to allow him to guide me. This guidance included me closing my eyes and just listening to his words—words that guided me into deep breathing, into embracing the power of each breath in and out. Without my conscious noticing, his words led me to complete stillness. Suddenly I heard him say, "Melissa, do you feel that?"

I had not realized until then that I had transformed from so much fear that it overwhelmed my body to the point that I physically vibrated us both, into a state of complete groundedness and calm, a transformation so powerful that I then just walked across to the end of the rope without hesitation. It was metamorphic, it was cathartic, and I had a natural high the rest of the day. But what I took with me—and still feel seven years later—was a newfound belief and trust in the power of breath.

When immersing yourself in nature isn't an option, and time is less abundant, there are alternative methods to have in your tool kit as well. Breathing is one of the most important things our body does and the ability to breathe with intention is a muscle most people underwork.

Breathwork can have a calming effect on several glands in the body, primarily through its influence on the autonomic nervous system. It can help lower the production of stress hormones, such as cortisol and adrenaline (which we will explore in Chapter 2) by promoting relaxation. It can influence the hypothalamic-pituitary-adrenal (HPA) axis, which plays a key role in stress response. It can help enhance relaxation and improve sleep quality, indirectly affecting melatonin production. As we embrace the things that give us a sense of groundedness, we also give ourselves the space, the stillness, and the courage for the deeper exploration needed to find our purpose through self-discovery.

As with many of the women I interviewed, we can find a deeper connection to purpose through meditation, breathwork, and yoga, as the stillness helps us connect with our higher self and make clearer choices. These practices help us deal with triggers and find peace and calm in challenging situations. Just as I found peace through breathwork during a tightrope walk, the power of breath can transform your state of mind.

The Interconnectedness: Intuition, Emotional Intelligence, and Mindfulness

As we reflect on the interconnectedness of intuition, emotional intelligence, and mindfulness, we can see that trusting our gut is not merely a theoretical notion but a deeply rooted cognitive and emotional process that has the power to transform our point of view on our lives. My experience, along with that of Shirley Ramos Roseman's and countless others, demonstrates that intuition is not random; it is the culmination of subconscious processing, past experiences, and heightened self-awareness. When we attune ourselves to these inner signals, we open doors to clarity, resilience, and, ultimately, our mental well-being.

Our reluctance to trust intuition often stems from societal conditioning that favors logic over instinct, the tangible over the abstract. However, as we see through scientific research—from Malcolm Gladwell's exploration of rapid cognition to William James's dual-process theory—intuition is just as valid as rational analysis, if not more so in moments of urgency. The brain's ability to synthesize information beyond our conscious awareness highlights the necessity of embracing this inner wisdom.

Yet intuition does not function in isolation. It is intimately tied to our emotional intelligence, which allows us to navigate our internal and external worlds with greater awareness. The higher one's EQ, the more attuned we are to our emotions, fostering a deeper connection with our intuition.

The ability to truly harness intuition requires more than just awareness—it also requires practice and discipline. Mindfulness can serve as the bridge between logic and intuition, creating space for clarity amid life's noise. Through mindfulness practices such as breathwork, meditation, and engagement with nature, we can strengthen our ability to listen to our inner selves. As Shirley discovered post-stroke and as I experienced on the tightrope four stories in the air at Miraval, mindfulness does not just offer moments of stillness; it sharpens our instincts and deepens our trust in them.

Breathwork, in particular, acts as a tool for recalibrating the nervous system, alleviating stress, and heightening our ability to sense subtle emotional and physical cues. The science behind breathwork and its impact on the autonomic nervous system (which we will further explore in Chapter 2) illustrates its ability to calm stress responses, enhancing our capacity for intuitive thought. When we engage in deep, intentional breathing, we allow ourselves to step out of fear, into trust, and into an alignment with our inner knowing.

Our intuition is always speaking to us, whether through a whisper of discomfort, a persistent thought, or an inexplicable knowing. The challenge lies not in its existence but in our willingness to listen, and to trust it.

Intuition in Business as Leaders: On a Path to Leadership

Ask an experienced CEO how they made a major decision, and their typical response is "intuition" or "gut feel." Yes, analysis also plays a role, but intuition was found to be a major or determining factor in 85% of 36 major CEO decisions that we studied.[10]

If intuition is our innate wisdom, and we develop an openness to listening to it and the accompanying signs it shows us, we not only find a transformation in how we live our personal lives, but we also heighten our potential in how we navigate ourselves as leaders. It gives us a deeper level of wisdom on planning for situations, our relationship with people, and—with practice—our innate intuitive abilities will become clearer and second nature (no pun intended). Another muscle we must practice is getting in tune with ourselves as individuals because as we uncover those layers and find foundational grounding in who we are, the more receptive we then become to the power of intuition.

When Nancy Berger, then chief revenue officer at Heart Magazines, left her career in publishing of more than 30 years, it wasn't because she had a solid plan for what was next but because she had an innate intuition it was time for something different. "It was a moment of combustion—I needed to do something personally purpose-forward," Nancy told me.

Nancy didn't just have a career in publishing; she had a track record of innovative thinking. She was and is known for seeing white space opportunities. She was always an "intrapreneur" with a legacy of birthing new ways to extend brands and revenue streams. She incepted the Marie Claire Power Trip, the Next Big Thing Pop-Up (which is how we met), and Cosmopolitan's Cosmo Trips Travel Product. She was an impact player and game changer, but eventually her work wasn't nourishing her soul the way it once had.

On a plane ride home from San Francisco in February 2023, her intuition stepped in to give her the clarity she needed to see that "it was time." As she worked on her cross-country flight, like she often did, she put a movie on in the background: *Mack & Rita* with Diane Keaton. The movie synopsis read, "The frustrated writer and influencer magically transforms into her future self: Aunt Rita. Freed from the constraints of other people's expectations, Rita comes into her own, becoming an unlikely social media sensation and sparking a tentative romance with Mack's adorable dog-sitter, Jack." When Rita is told, "You have been invited to the Marie Claire Power Trip, the most important trip for Women in the World," Nancy's inner being heard more than just an actor speaking. She intuitively heard her larger purpose personified; she heard, "What I do is bigger than just thinking about magazines and media. I connect people and opportunities and new places that can make a difference." By the time the plane landed, Nancy had drafted her resignation letter and a LinkedIn post that literally went viral with more support than she could have imagined.[11]

Today, Nancy is thriving in her new direction with her new company Swag (Start with a Good . . . idea, product, story, mission, purpose). Her clients include Tribeca Festival, Art Basel, Daily Beast, Katie Couric Media, and many more. But more pointedly, Nancy is living her purpose pivot. She is leaning into her driving force and authentic passions of being a connector and her gift of identifying areas of growth and innovation across mediums and industries. For her, working with clients is about starting with a good idea, vision, and so on, to unlock the greatness in it. Trusting her intuition not only let Nancy pivot her point of view on her purpose, but also enabled her to nourish her soul in new ways as a difference maker.

When We Trust Intuition

Different from cognitive reasoning, intuition comes from paying attention to our emotions and being open to them. Typically, as leaders, we rely on facts and information, but that can also often be a circular conversation when depending on that alone, because there is usually incomplete information or conflicting points of view on the information at hand. When one can lean into and trust intuition as the additive layer, that trust becomes a valuable leadership competency.

As we close this chapter, we see that intuition, often dismissed as abstract or unreliable, is a profound force that connects our mind, body, and emotions in ways that logic cannot always explain. Whether through the life-changing experiences shared, the insights of my story or that of Shirley Ramos and Nancy Berger, or the scientific backing from pioneers like William James and Malcolm Gladwell, this chapter illustrates that trusting your gut is more than a cliché—it's a skill that can be honed and can lead to a lifeline to self-awareness and purpose.

In Chapter 4, I will cover more about our personal PI (predictable indexes) and further explore our path to finding purpose, both personally and professionally. It is through self-discovery and exploration that we can discover our tendencies, our drivers, our desires—how they serve us, and how at times they do not—and where we find our sense of meaning. All of these layers contribute to our level of acceptance of our gut feeling and intuition.

As a first exercise in our collective journey, here are some ways we can not only embrace a connection with intuition, or decipher that "gut feeling," but allow the power of it into our lives in a spectrum of ways:

- **Be mindful.** Notice the signs or feelings and allow yourself to feel them.
- **Trust.** Give yourself the permission of acceptance. Avoid preconceived judgment and instead allow in your instinct.
- **Allow for exploration.** When the signs seep in, ask yourself what it means and how you can channel the energy.
- **Give yourself stillness.** Find time to step away or step out to find the space where you can silence the chatter and ruminate in quiet contemplation, maybe with the surroundings of nature and its elements or even mundane task.

Chapter 1 Contributors:

Shirley Ramos Roseman, Jennifer Walsh, Nancy Berger, Tai Beauchamp

2

Understanding the Science of Stress and Womanhood

Decoding the Physiological and Emotional Impacts of Stress

Weeks after returning home from surgery, my body was still working very hard to mend and heal from my intestines being untwisted, part of my colon being removed, and another part of my colon being glued internally to my inner wall. And when the body is physically healing, and in this case re-appending, a whole lot of other internal reshuffling also takes place. I think my husband will never forget me saying to him, "I have to be honest; I hate you today and everything you do annoys me and there is little I can do about feeling this way and I am pretty sure I am going to feel this way for the next two weeks at best."

It was not the nicest moment, but when you have the right partner, brutal and transparent honesty can help break down walls and create support. Because what I was really saying was this: "Please be helpful while I am trying to understand and navigate what exactly is happening to me internally, a hormonal process I recognize was evolving inside of me and over which I had little control."

Post-surgery, I had to take it slow for three months, per doctor's orders, to ensure I fully healed. I felt a constant tension between embracing decompression and the ongoing flight-or-fight stress response that fueled my every day pre-January 10, and experiencing what felt like a roller coaster of hormonal changes that I had zero control over. It's an interesting study to experience what happens to the body as stress seeps out of it. Our free-flowing thoughts find more space, our muscles become less sore from what happens to the body under constant mental tension, we laugh more, and we gain an appreciation for things we put in the background.

In this chapter, I explore the science of stress for us as individuals and as women. The chapter is presented in three sections. The first focuses on these questions: What is the difference between positive stress and negative stress? What do our bodies release in those various states and what are the impacts of those releases? What is the impact of cortisol, dopamine, serotonin? Is it possible to create change through understanding? In the second section, I layer in the female factor and our continuous hormonal changes, which add additional complexities to our bodies' relationship to stress, both mentally and physically, through an exploration of the relationship between stress and estrogen, estrogen and perimenopause, menopause, and beyond. And as we gain insight around stress and the female factor, in the third section I weave in insights from nutritionists, fitness experts, and female founders from companies such as HerMD, Womaness, and Nutritious Life, who share information about how we can lean into the opportunity of healthy aging.

This may be my longest chapter, but as I researched through group conversations, one-on-one interviews, and tireless readings and audiobooks, I found myself down many rabbit holes of information. And time and time again I found myself intrigued by findings, the recognition of the intuitive aspect of self-care and the fact that we ignore most of it or at least deprioritize it. I am hopeful, though, that through learning we can begin to see why understanding our bodies and giving priority to what they need becomes so critical to our health, well-being, and ability as leaders.

The Tension Between Positive Stress and Negative Stress

> "We literally make babies, and still we feel the need to always 'power through' and juggle so much."
>
> **—Sarah Kugelman, founder of Skyn Iceland and All Golden**

Entrepreneur Sarah Kugelman has built two successful beauty brands that have become synonymous with key inflection points in the beauty industry—digital and wellness. Prior to her journey into entrepreneurship, she worked at some of the industry's leading beauty companies, including L'Oreal, Bath & Body Works, and Estee Lauder, where she held P&L responsibility and drove brand strategy, omni-channel marketing, and product development. With her vast experience, she has not only incepted her own companies—one of which was acquired—but she also has two decades of board experience, having served on two corporate boards.

But looking back at her younger self, in her 30s Sarah didn't often see that what she was doing was enough. She would power through very high levels of stress and push it aside, even at the cost of wearing down her own immune system. Her weakened immune system led her to come down with a case of chicken pox at an uncommonly late age. This was followed by a respiratory infection, and ultimately over time her immune system continued to deteriorate, until one day she collapsed. When the whole room would not stop spinning around, life stepped in and made her pause—a pause that forced her to stop working and spend hours a day in a dark room for three months to regain alignment.

Even when she had the signs that her body was shutting down, Sarah still did not give herself the permission to pause. She was fueled by adrenaline, or what seemed like positive stress. But as many of us know, when we are on that constant rush, the lines begin to blur between positive and negative stressors, and we get accustomed to just reacting to our flight-or-fight "power-through" reaction, regardless of the stressor. For Sarah, life forced her to stop powering when she worked her adrenal glands so hard that her body just shut down from fatigue.

Stress is not always a bad thing. It's an intrinsic aspect of life; it's what establishes our natural response to demands, challenges, and opportunities. And it happens when those incoming demands, challenges, and opportunities disrupt our natural state of equilibrium. For many of us—especially women in leadership roles, on entrepreneurial paths, and/or juggling motherhood—that is pretty often.

When we are healthy and well balanced, our body is well equipped to handle our natural stress system. In a healthy stress response, the brain sends signals to a pair of glands located in the abdomen, triggering the release of stress hormones. These hormones (adrenaline, cortisol, DHEA, and more) then enter the bloodstream and travel throughout the body to create changes such as slowed digestion, elevated blood pressure, dilated pupils, an increased heart rate and breathing rate, increased mental focus, and more.[1] The danger comes when we overwork our response system and our response begins to go haywire. Over time, if the system is triggered too often, the body starts to confuse what is an appropriate reason to elicit a response and what is not. For example, do you ever find yourself getting more worked up or upset about something than you should but are unsure why? Do you find it harder and harder to be patient about little things, and looking back think to yourself, did that really need to make me so upset or annoyed? According to Dr. Alexandra MacKillop, DC, this happens when the body begins to trigger stress hormones to be released during times when no stress trigger exists; likewise, in situations in which a person might expect to feel triggered, the body fails to produce the appropriate stress response.

In instances such as Sarah's, adrenal failure or adrenal insufficiency occurs when the adrenal glands (small glands located above the kidneys) do not produce enough essential hormones, such as cortisol and aldosterone, which are crucial for regulating our metabolism, blood pressure, immune responses, and stress adaptation. In severe cases, an "adrenal crisis" can occur, presenting as shock, severe dehydration, confusion, and/or dangerously low blood sugar and blood pressure, which requires immediate medical intervention.

Let's take a look at breaking down the difference between positive stress and negative stress.

Positive stress can feel exciting and keep us motivated. It can improve our performance and can drive us to take on healthy challenges. If we take a vacation somewhere that is a new, unknown adventure, if we start a new role or a new job, if we move somewhere new or purchase a home, these can all elicit positive stress responses. For me, I experience positive stress any time I get on stage for a keynote presentation or a media appearance. I get a little shaky (sometimes even with goosebumps), I have to regulate my breath, and I have to remind myself, "You got this." But what my body is releasing once I am on stage is a positive rush of adrenaline because although I might be nervous, I love what I get to do—educate and share my knowledge in a value exchange with my audience, and it's extremely fulfilling. That high for me is my natural dopamine fix and a "modulation of the dopaminergic reward system is necessary for monitoring and selecting the optimal process for coping with stressful situations."[2]

Positive stress, also known as eustress, plays a vital role in promoting growth, resilience, and overall well-being. It acts as a catalyst for improved cognitive and physical[3] performance by providing a sense of urgency and focus and stimulates problem-solving abilities and productivity. Numerous studies[4] further suggest that manageable stress levels can enhance mental alertness, leading to optimal functioning in high-stakes situations as well as encouraging creative thinking and innovation. This level of thinking also fosters the development of a growth mindset,[5] one that can reframe obstacles as opportunities. Eustress also facilitates our personal and professional growth by encouraging us to step out of our comfort zones, fostering strong social bonds when conquering unknown situations in groups, and it has been linked to positive health outcomes, including enhanced immune function and overall well-being.[6] Positive stress also contributes to mental wellness by promoting optimism and self-efficacy, which we will explore more later in this chapter.

For Sarah, despite her collapse, her journey with her relationship to stress has led to extremely positive outcomes as well, like increased mental focus and a surge of positive adrenaline—experienced when launching her two science-backed beauty brands, driven by her opportunity to home in on her intentional purpose of bringing science and beauty together in an accessible way.

At some point, Sarah's body went into overload, and when that happens to any of us—when a human body is exposed to stress with too much frequency, at durations that push too long, without space for a decompression that allows the equilibrium to resent—the body's stress response falls into a state of dysfunction. By learning to find pauses that give reconciliation and a recentering, we can allow the attributes of positive stress to be growth drivers for us.

Negative stress, on the other hand, is driven by sources of distress rather than the things that fuel us. And instead of being a driver to improved performance or increased focus, it leads to things like anxiety and decreased performance. For example, it appears during times like overscheduling yourself with excessive demands at work that steal your energy, losing a job, being in unhealthy relationships, or feeling marginalized—things that don't drive you forward but rather cause dissatisfaction and apathy. These stressors can begin to impact our mental health, especially when they occur with frequent occurrence and/or over sustained periods of time, and we begin to lose our ability for positive resets.

If you search online for "negative impacts of stress on the body," these results will float to the top: insomnia, headaches, chest pain, depression, fatigue, irritability, anxiety, high blood pressure, and obesity. And while many of us have felt these in varying degrees, our instinct is often to "power through it," rather than pause and ask, "Is this healthy for me? What can I do differently?"

It might seem mind boggling, but it wasn't until 1936 that János Hugo Bruno "Hans" Selye coined the term "stress" and made it his mission to demystify the term that it began to be more deeply studied. "Everyone knows what stress is, but nobody really knows about stress."[7] It was then that he also began to observe the connection between stress symptoms and chronic illnesses. It's also been evidenced through his work that stress is a crucial factor in psychopathology, particularly the development of depression. And while the terms "positive stress" and "negative stress" don't appear in his research, the study of stress resulting in the loss of pleasure or a lack of motivation as core features of depression are cited.

> "The signs that show up externally are often the aftermath of what has already been happening internally."
>
> **—Tai Beauchamp, founder, Morning Mindset with Tai**

Negative stress, or "distress," is a pervasive phenomenon that, when unmanaged, can erode an individual's well-being across multiple dimensions. Distress can overwhelm our body's ability to cope, leading to significant consequences for mental, physical, and social health. Chronic exposure to stressors, such as job insecurity or relationship conflicts, can impair cognitive functions like memory, focus, and decision-making.[8] It also often leads to what feels like emotional instability, not too dissimilar to the example I shared with my husband, when I could literally feel myself manifesting irritability and exacerbated mood swings that were straining my personal relationship. Negative stress triggers the body's fight-or-flight response, releasing hormones like cortisol (addressed in the next section), and prolonged activation of this stress response can result in conditions such as hypertension, cardiovascular disease, and immune system suppression.

We all have a relationship with stress in our lives; it's fairly impossible to exist without it. But the key is understanding how chronic stress can exacerbate negative emotional patterns and reduce coping capacity. Finding ways to have a healthy balance of positive and negative stressors can be achieved in the lives we create for ourselves.

What Is Cortisol?

> When we experience stress, our bodies release hormones like epinephrine (adrenaline), cortisol, and norepinephrine.
>
> —**Body Logic MD**

Cortisol, known as the primary stress hormone, increases sugar in the bloodstream, enhancing the brain's use of glucose and increasing the availability of substances in the body that repair tissues. It also slows functions that would be nonessential or harmful in a fight-or-flight situation. It changes immune system responses and suppresses the digestive system, the reproductive system and growth processes. This complex natural alarm system also communicates with the brain regions that control mood, motivation and fear[9]

Three months post-surgery, when my body regulated back, I went to Next Health and took that full-panel blood test that Mona Sharma guided me to do back in 2023 (as I mentioned in my introduction). One of the areas of focus in my test were my stressors. The morning of my test, when my day had seemingly just begun, I had already been bombarded by work emails, chased my daughter out of bed to get her ready for school, taken two trains to the city, and got lost finding the entrance to the lab, all on an empty stomach. Basically by my test time of 8:30 a.m., I had already had a mini day in itself before the visit even began. And when the results of my blood panel came in, guess what—my cortisol levels were "oddly high."

Well, if cortisol communicates mood, my mood definitely had some stress to start my day. Nothing out of the ordinary per se, but it was a lesson in how I was receiving my day, how I was allowing it to manifest internally, how perhaps I could approach "taking my breath differently." It was enlightening to see a score so high, so early in the day. Were my reactions to the little things out of whack due to the sustained levels of stress I was managing throughout my every day, and my perpetually conditioned flight-or-fight response?

When evenly balanced, our body uses cortisol for several important functions, such as decreasing inflammation, lifting our energy levels, maintaining a healthy blood pressure, and managing how the body processes carbs, fats, and proteins. But seeing a cortisol level so high, so early in my day, made me attune to understanding that the more frequently we are activating our stress response and exposure to cortisol hormones, the more it begins to disrupt our body's process and affiliation with stress, whether it's positive or negative.

According to the Mayo Clinic,[10] when we develop an unbalanced relationship to stress for long or frequent durations of time we can experience:

- Anxiety
- Depression
- Digestive problems

- Headaches
- Muscle tension and pain
- Heart disease, heart attack, high blood pressure and stroke
- Sleep problems
- Weight gain
- Problems with memory and focus

Cortisol has the ability to impact numerous organs in our bodies; thus understanding our triggers and being proactive in how we handle our response to stress is critical. As a hormone, it also helps regulate our body's response to stress—feels kind of counterintuitive, but also highlights its significance. Almost all tissues in our body have glucocorticoid receptors, and because of this, cortisol can affect nearly every organ system, including the nervous system, the immune system, cardiovascular system, respiratory system, reproductive system, musculoskeletal system, and integumentary system (skin, hair, nails, glands and nerves).[11]

It's a significant impact many of us underestimate. And as we feel less out of control of our responses, it's an even bigger reminder to make sure we proactively pause. Our bodies are telling us our ability to reset to homeostasis is off, and the further we stray from a healthy immune system, the more challenging that reset becomes.

> "I never focused on self-care in a very meaningful way. Yes, I got my nails and hair done, but I wasn't making myself better from the inside."
>
> **—Melissa Guerrero, VP/DMM, cosmetics retail executive**

What Is Cortisol Detox?

If one thing is for sure, once you do an Instagram search for the word "cortisol," a whole lot of cortisol detox programs start to fill the feed. It can be overwhelming, but what does it really mean?

According to numerous medical sources—such as WebMD, Cleveland Clinic, and Next Health—normal ranges for most tests that measure cortisol levels are:

6 a.m. to 8 a.m.: 10 to 20 micrograms per deciliter (mcg/dL)

Around 4 p.m.: 3 to 10 mcg/dL

(Note that the normal ranges are slightly different for children and the elderly.)

For the saliva test, the normal range for adults is:

10.2 to 27.3 nanograms per milliliter (ng/mL) in the morning

2 to 4.1 ng/mL at night

If you have lower than normal or extremely high levels of cortisol, you could turn to medical treatment to lower your cortisol levels. And while you should check with your doctor regardless before embarking on any detox, as you look at what it entails for someone outside of the extreme ranges, you observe at its simplest, it's about investing and prioritizing best practices for healthier living. Some ideas you can take control of on your own:

- Consistent, quality sleep
- Regular exercise
- A balanced diet
- Flush out toxins (i.e., stay well hydrated)
- Stress management

Cortisol detoxification is a concept tied to reducing stress and optimizing cortisol levels in the body. Incorporating regular exercise, sufficient sleep, and a balanced diet (which we explore later in this chapter) in our lives can support healthy cortisol levels. Mindfulness practices like meditation are also beneficial. So what holds us back from prioritizing healthier living as a best practice, just like we prioritize anything else?

What Is Dopamine?

As defined in the *Harvard Business Review*, "Dopamine is most notably involved in helping us feel pleasure as part of the brain's reward system. Sex, shopping, smelling cookies baking in the oven—all these things can trigger dopamine release, or a 'dopamine rush.'"[12]

We have all heard the term "dopamine rush." In comparison to cortisol, dopamine is often referred to as one of our "feel-good" hormones, creating feelings of pleasure and providing motivation to pursue enjoyable activities. It is a neurotransmitter produced in the brain, transmitting signals between nerve cells.

This "chemical messenger" doesn't just impact the brain but communicates with the entire body, influencing a wide range of activities—for example our movement, memory, and cognition. It is also part of a group of hormones called catecholamines, which also includes epinephrine (adrenaline) and norepinephrine. These hormones share a similar molecular structure and are produced by the adrenal glands, which sit atop our kidneys. Dopamine is also released by the hypothalamus in the brain and is critical to various bodily functions.[13]

In addition to being central to our reward system, it's also a mechanism to encourage survival behaviors like eating, drinking, and reproduction. It is thus often associated with things like sex, and when engaged in pleasurable activities, the brain releases large amounts of dopamine, creating a positive feeling that drives us to repeat the experience—for example, going after that whole bag of your guilty-pleasure Doritos versus just a chip or two, or that whole chocolate cake.

The right balance of dopamine leads to feelings of happiness, motivation, alertness, and focus. Low dopamine levels can cause tiredness, lack of motivation, and unhappiness, while high dopamine levels may bring euphoria, increased energy, and a high sex drive. Understanding what triggers the right release of varying levels can give us better stress management. All in all, it takes a concerted effort to keep hormonal levels in balance.

Our Genetic Disposition to Stress

> "Man is not worried by real problems so much as by his imagined anxieties about real problems."
>
> **—Epictetus**

There is scientific evidence that genetic variation in the serotonin, HPA axis, and oxytocin systems moderates the effects of psychosocial vulnerability markers on the generation of proximal, dependent life events.[14] Over decades, there have been numerous studies between biomarkers and various stress- and anxiety-related diagnoses.

As individuals, as we better learn about ourselves and the differences of positive and negative stress and about the various hormones that are released in our blood streams, we also benefit from the awareness of our own genetic dispositions. For me, investing in my full blood panel tests has been extremely enlightening. Through such tests we gain greater appreciation of the fact that we are not all at the same starting place, that various imbalances simply genetically exist, and the way our bodies transport hormones and nutrients vary. This information gives us a new position of understanding that is empowering.

Biomarkers, for one, are measurable traits in our blood, body fluids, and tissues that help us understand various aspects of our health. Also known as molecular markers or signature molecules, biomarkers can indicate normal functions, disease presence, or when something is amiss in the body. They are also useful for gauging how well we respond to elements put into our bodies and released within our bodies.

As humans, we are more wired to remember negative experiences or traumas over positive moments or celebrations. As we experience more traumas throughout our lives, they begin to impact and reshape how our system responds to the things that stress us or we perceive to "threaten" us. Some of us are more wired for optimism and some more for pessimism, and the jury is still out on how much of the balance is attributed to nature versus nurture. Our optimism characteristics allow us to thrive through challenges and setbacks, while our pessimistic side sees threats as impossibilities. Add to this all, as women our hormones rebalance not just on a monthly but also on a yearly basis, and the pendulum of our moods not only shifts but can feel out of our control, and this too impacts our relationship to stress.

While this is not a deep dive into psychoanalysis, it's relevant and educational to understand we all have unique biomarkers and dispositions and we have environmental contributors that can either add to or alleviate stress, but our one undeniable commonality is that we all have a relationship with stress. The key is how we manage it.

Back to the Relationship Between Stress and Illness

Due to its connection to all the systems listed in this chapter, our relationship to stress has significant impacts on our well-being. Too often we hear of a person falling victim to a heart attack "out of nowhere" and way too young. Our cardiovascular health can be highly impacted by triggers of stress that happen at too high a frequency and/or too prolonged a duration, especially because our bodies can only withstand an elevated heart rate or increased blood pressure for so long without causing eventual damage. Consider the musculoskeletal system, for example, and think about how often you find yourself clenching your jaw, scowling your face, tensing your shoulders, holding a tight fist. Over time, this sustained muscle tension leads to aches and pains and then eventually escalates to things like spasms, twitches, headaches, and other nagging and painful ailments and we feel like our bodies are just breaking down. Women are also not strangers to inflammation and digestive issues, with many of us powering through stomach issues not just due to stress hormones but also as we navigate menstrual cycles. The stress hormones that slow the release of stomach acid and the emptying of the stomach (in preparation for the flight-or-fight response) also stimulate the colon.[15]

I can raise my hand for many of the things I just listed—a bulging disk in my neck, borderline TMJ, and most recently a twisted intestine and colon issues. Being more informed and aware has been educational and revealing.

> "Growing up, my mom was one of the healthiest people I knew, so seeing her diagnosed with dementia has been a profound wake-up call. It's made me realize, in a much deeper way, the critical importance of self-care as a priority, not just a 'nice to have.' As an entrepreneur for the past two decades, I am now making it a key part of my business approach. This isn't just about scheduling a workout class; I'm exploring things like group outings for blood panel work with my teams."
>
> **—Stacy Igel, founder and CCO of BOY MEETS GIRL® and author of *Embracing the Calm in the Chaos***

Here are some ways you can begin to create a better balance and relationship with your response to stress:

- **Identify the feeling.** Note when the stress you are feeling is positive or negative and see if you can identify patterns.
- **Learn to limit your stress patterns.** Through identification you can also begin to chart how you create a positive shift.
- **Develop mindfulness techniques.** Find an app to guide you so you don't hold the full burden of execution, whether that's meditation, deep breathing exercises, and or techniques for progressive muscle relaxation.
- **Learn how to delegate.** Time management is often spoken of, but we can only optimize our time so much unless we are willing to share the load.
- **Leave space to move the body:** Start with a commitment of 10 minutes a day, take a call off camera and walk and talk. If you aren't screensharing, they don't really have to see you or buddy up—so find that friend or colleague to take a walking meeting with.
- **Ditch cocktails.** Instead, make your happy hour with a friend a physical activity, or maybe even get that manicure you think you can't squeeze into your week.

Positive Stress and Leadership

> "When you are blazing trails, you are going to burn if you don't find space for arrested pause and reconciliation."
>
> **—Tai Beauchamp, founder of Morning Mindset with Tai**

As with my own journey, the silver lining is what it taught Sarah, and what it can help us all channel. It led her to find her higher purpose, not too dissimilar from the experience of Shirley and Nancy in Chapter 1. As women we are often multitasking, are highly driven to achieve, and can put a tremendous amount of pressure on ourselves to deliver in numerous arenas at the same time.

Once we gain the ability to recognize the difference between positive stress and negative stress, we can be more proactive in determining what we make more space for and what we make less space for, and we can create positive boundaries. This is also a powerful attribute when we think of our ability as leaders, especially because reclaiming time becomes one of our most valuable assets.

We often wait for something monumental, like a health scare, before we pause, reflect, and discover purpose. The reality is that many of us are actually extremely well versed in prioritization when it comes to business we manage, whether that be as entrepreneurs, in corporate America, or even at home. We can time-manage the crap out of any day or week, we can compartmentalize, we can push the bullshit out of the way, ensuring that key things are accomplished and in a hierarchy of importance, but often we fail to do so for ourselves.

If the lack of enough time is a driver of negative stress, then understanding how to open up space for the things of most impact and gratification for us as individuals can give us the ability to be more in control of our days and gain better control of our personal stress management. (We will dive further into finding our purpose in Chapter 4, because purpose serves as a North Star to declutter our lives to make room for positive stressors and less space for the negative ones.)

By doing the work ourselves, as leaders we also have the opportunity to be role models for others, giving permission to making space for positive stressors and less space for the negative ones. And as we begin to build our own tool kit, we not only have a healthier balance for ourselves, but it also equips us to manage more resilient, thriving teams.

The Female Layer and Stress: The Relationship Between Stress and Estrogen

Earlier we examined the relationship between stress and cortisol. As women it's also important we understand the complexities not only of stress but the role of estrogen and how it impacts our mental and physical state.

According to the American Psychological Association, women are more likely than men to report having a great deal of stress that is characterized as an 8, 9, or 10 on a 10-point scale.[16] That's nothing to roll an eye at, and especially as we look at the relationship between stress and hormones.

The body produces three forms of the estrogen hormone—estradiol, estriol, and estrone—which shift throughout life. Estrogen is central to female reproductive health that also plays a crucial role in overall health, particularly in brain function. It supports cognitive health, mood management, and protects neural structures, aiding in learning, memory, and executive functions. Estrogen, especially estradiol, promotes neuron growth and neuroplasticity, allowing the brain to adapt and change. Estrogen levels naturally decline with age, with the decline accelerating after a hysterectomy or due to autoimmune conditions, impacting brain health and emotional well-being.

The relationship between cortisol and estrogen is intricate and significantly influenced by stress. The body is wired to regulate cortisol levels as we recover from a state of stress, but when we are under a constant state or chronic state of stress, not only do our cortisol levels rise, but more of it also gets into our blood stream. When a person experiences chronic stress, the body continuously produces cortisol, and this becomes particularly important for women because high levels of cortisol for sustained periods of time can disrupt the menstrual cycle by affecting ovulation—the monthly release of an egg. Typically, during this phase, a woman's body ramps up estrogen production to prepare for potential fertilization. However, elevated cortisol levels can interfere with this process, potentially leading to reduced estrogen levels and irregular menstrual cycles.

On the flip side, high levels of estrogen can impact cortisol production. Specifically, estrogen increases the concentration of cortisol-binding globulin (CBG), which can alter how cortisol functions in the body. Estrogen also plays a role in modulating brain networks, stress response, and emotional regulation. During periods of low estrogen, women can also be at greater risk for experiencing symptoms of depression, which may occur because estrogen affects serotonin function in the brain.[17]

It's a dynamic interplay between highlighting the complexities of women's health, particularly under stress. Fun, right?

As we piece more of the puzzle together, here is a list from Rockville ObGyn[18] of symptoms that can be caused by hormonal imbalances in women:

- Heavy or frequent periods
- Stopped or missed periods
- Hair loss or thinning
- Pain during sex
- Vaginal dryness/atrophy
- Weight gain
- Night sweats
- Skin tags
- Darkening of the skin in the neck creases, groin, or underneath the breasts
- Acne on the face, chest, or upper back
- Excessive hair growth on the face or chin

What Is Perimenopause?

"I think of it as reverse puberty."

—Dr. Meg Hainer, MD, ob-gyn

Perimenopause is a natural phase in a woman's life that occurs as the ovaries gradually cease their function. It's a phase common to all women, but still being demystified scientifically. It's the precursor to menopause that your mom had no idea about and therefore likely didn't educate you about.

During this time, ovulation may become unpredictable and eventually stop altogether. Women often experience longer menstrual cycles and irregular flow leading up to their final period. These changes are accompanied by various symptoms, all stemming from the shifting levels of hormones in the body. Until recently, this part of a woman's life was barely talked about. We either had our periods or we were in menopause. However, this period of perimenopause is pretty significant in a woman's life.

According to WebMD, perimenopause typically starts 8 to 10 years before menopause and usually occurs in our mid-40s, although it can start even earlier. And it ends once you have gone 12 months without having a period.

Not too dissimilar to the list from Rockville ObGyn, according to John Hopkins study of medicine, these are the most common symptoms of perimenopause:[19]

- Mood changes
- Changes in sexual desire
- Trouble concentrating
- Trouble with memory, aka brain fog
- Headaches
- Night sweats
- Hot flashes
- Cold flashes
- Vaginal dryness
- Trouble with sleep
- Joint and muscle aches
- Heavy sweating
- Having to pee often
- PMS-like symptoms

There is still so much for us as women to learn from this stage of transition; however, research indicates that perimenopause can also significantly heighten stress levels in women due to hormonal fluctuations and the physical and emotional changes associated with this transitional phase. And as we look at the complex relationship between estrogen and stress, studies have also shown that the decrease in estrogen can lead to increased anxiety and mood disturbances, making women more susceptible to stress.[20] Conversely, chronic stress can exacerbate perimenopausal symptoms, creating a feedback loop where stress affects hormone levels, which in turn influences mood and well-being.

Hormonal Change and Anxiety

During perimenopause, many of us experience a heightened relationship with anxiety, which can deeply affect how we respond to stress.

This increase in anxiety often stems from the substantial hormonal shifts occurring in the body at this stage. As estrogen levels drop, symptoms like hot flashes, poor sleep quality, and a racing mind with trouble focusing and concentrating become common, creating a cycle that can further amplify anxiety. And as our bodies go through this transition, three key neurotransmitters—serotonin (our "happiness hormone"), dopamine (the "feel good" brain chemicals), and norepinephrine (our "flight-or-fight response")—are significantly impacted, further influencing mood and emotional regulation.[21]

Serotonin helps promote feelings of calmness and happiness, contributing to emotional stability and well-being. When serotonin levels are low, it can lead to increased irritability, making a person more prone to feelings of crankiness and frustration. This neurotransmitter's balance is essential for maintaining a positive mood and overall emotional health. In addition to mood, serotonin is key for sleep; it plays a role in both sleep initiation and sleep maintenance. It affects our body's sleep-wake cycle by interacting with other neurotransmitters that regulate arousal and rest. When we don't get enough sleep, our tolerance for stressors begin to change, as well as our ability to remember things and focus, which compounds our stress levels.

Dopamine, as mentioned earlier, is also modulated by estrogen levels. Lower dopamine levels can lead to noticeable changes in mood, reducing our ability to concentrate and decreasing overall energy. Norepinephrine, the neurotransmitter linked to the body's fight-or-flight response, can become imbalanced during perimenopause and menopause, contributing to elevated blood pressure and heightened feelings of anxiety. These fluctuations can sometimes make us feel as though we are experiencing panic attacks, because the body's stress response is more easily triggered during this time.

Menopause

There is no concrete designation for the onset of menopause, but doctors generally consider that someone is in menopause after 12 consecutive months without a period.[22] While many of us have been taught that we will one day hit menopause, what we are beginning to more widely understand is that our awareness of the shorter duration of transitions we undergo in perimenopause and post-menopause are just as important. Perimenopause signifies when our estrogen production fluctuates most and menopause and post-menopause are when our estrogen production levels out.

Not too dissimilar to perimenopause, in menopause we can experience hot flashes, vaginal atrophy, cardiac effects (such as dizziness, numbness, tingling, heart palpitations), and mood changes (like irritability, lack of feeling ourselves, and sleep disturbances). There is still a tremendous amount of demystification needed when it comes to understanding the changes the body goes through in this phase of life. Initiatives like *The M Factor: Shredding the Silence on Menopause*[23] are sharing the stories of doctors who dedicate themselves to deeper research and women becoming more open about sharing their journey's, helping to shine a light on the impact this has on a woman's mental and physical well-being.

Menopause still remains a taboo topic in many cultures, leaving women uninformed and unprepared for the transition. Doctors and women going through their own journeys and sharing more publicly, such as Tamsen Fadal, Drew Barrymore, Halle Berry, Naomi Watts, and others, are slowly helping to shed societal norms that stigmatize natural biological processes, advocating for open conversations to empower women with knowledge.

Something we can begin to understand that allows us to find empowerment is that menopause factually has an impact on our mind and body. It's not in our imagination, and the more we talk about it with others and find support systems and resources, the better we understand these transitional periods of our lives. When it is layered on top of the stressors around us, we become more equipped with a deeper level of understanding, especially when and if we have moments when we feel overwhelmed. The reality is that our bodies are going through an internal evolution while we are trying to handle and cope with external factors.

The Opportunity of Healthy Aging

"Longevity starts at age 30."

—Sally Mueller, co-founder of Womaness

I first was introduced to the company Womaness several years ago, when a package was mailed to me that included vaginal moisturizer, a vibrator, and an eye opener. I understood the eye opener, but my reaction was "Why in the world would I be sent this package? I am not in menopause." (This is how the company marketed themselves at the time.) What I hadn't realized then was that I was actually already in perimenopause and many of these products were extremely relevant to me. Since then, the company has been positioning itself as one that modernizes healthy aging and is slowly taking a more holistic approach to what they offer women with a more solutions-oriented mindset versus a product company. They look at the skin and body, sexual wellness, and nutrition through supplements.

As we put the puzzle pieces of this three-part chapter together and begin to see the ties between what stress releases in our bodies, the role of hormones, its impact on sleep, the brain, and mental wellness, we also start to see there are many aspects we can lean into in terms of empowering ourselves with things we can take control off that bring our minds and bodies into a more positive state. Among others, these aspects include muscle mass, bone density, our nutrition, natural ways to "re-shock the system" like cold plunges, and the power of sleep and sex.

Movement and Strength Training

> "Being physical taught me to respect my body for what it offers me, and the gifts it gives me. For my students, I don't allow just two-pound weights; we create exercises and movement to feel strong."
>
> **—Marlyn Ortiz, professional dancer, former personal trainer for Madonna**

One area that tends to be of greatest surprise to women in terms of fitness and exercise is the rapid loss of muscle mass and the care needed around bone density as we approach perimenopause and menopause. Throughout these life stages, women often experience a marked decline in muscle mass due to hormonal changes. These changes are especially due to the drop in estrogen levels, which is a vital hormone for maintaining muscle health because it facilitates muscle protein synthesis and sustains muscle stem cell activity. When estrogen levels fall, the body undergoes an accelerated loss of muscle mass, or sarcopenia, starting during perimenopause and becoming more pronounced post-menopause

The rate of muscle loss, typically 3–8% per decade after the age of 30, increases post-menopause, often is accompanied by an increase in fat mass.[24] These changes can reduce our physical strength, impair mobility, and increase the risk of metabolic disorders. Muscle mass and strength are also particularly critical for overall health and injury prevention, because muscle supports bone health and metabolic functions. Strength training and protein intake can help counteract this decline. Through preventive exercise, strength-building movement, and diet, we can stay ahead of the impact.

I often follow my friend Maryln's workouts because she is in phenomenal shape. She has danced her whole life, and traveled on tour with the likes of Taylor Swift, Black Eyed Peas, Madonna, and Brittany Spears. She was Madonna's personal trainer for years and if you look her up you will see the embodiment of *fit*. And yet she too shares her story of rapidly losing muscle mass once she hit her 40s. For her, movement has been a blessing, a way to release, a way to conquer parts of herself and have a deeper connection with her physical and mental well-being. Through her work in movement and exercise, she is more actively bridging both mental and physical wellness.

She shares the increasing importance of incorporating resistance exercises, a protein-rich diet, and other supportive practices like balance and flexibility training as we approach perimenopause in order to improve quality of life and physical resilience during and after menopause.

Strength training plays a crucial role in enhancing muscle strength and maintaining functional mobility as women age. Increased muscle mass not only supports our daily activities but also contributes to better posture and balance, reducing the likelihood of falls and injuries. Moreover, strength training helps regulate metabolism, which tends to slow down as we age, and it can counteract the natural muscle loss that inevitably occurs.[25]

Beyond physical benefits, lifting weights positively influences the nervous system. Studies indicate that strength training enhances neuromuscular function, improving our motor control, coordination, and overall nervous system efficiency.[26] These benefits also help maintain agility and reduce the decline in cognitive and motor skills that comes as we age.

Whether it's weightlifting, resistance band workouts, or bodyweight exercises, if we can also improve bone density, reduce the risk of osteoporosis and fractures, and enhance metabolism to better manage weight gain and improve overall metabolic health, we can feel mentally stronger as well. Here are some techniques that can positively impact our nervous system, especially when our body is in biological transitions:

- A walk in the park
- Metabolic activities, even if for just 10 minutes
- Natural exposures to vitamin D
- Time with a pet
- Disconnection from social media

Nutrition and Supplements

> "If your gut health isn't in check, you may lack sufficient good bacteria, which can impact serotonin production—key for balancing mood and managing stress."
>
> **—Keri Glassman, MS, RD, CDN, founder of Nutritious Life**

One thing that I have gained very intimate knowledge about post-January 10, 2024, in addition to trusting my gut, is the value and importance of gut health. Our gut links to everything; if our body had a second brain, many would consider it to be our gut. And, like stress, our gut also links to estrogen, and when we have an unhealthy or leaky gut, we lose both nutrients and estrogen.

Keri Glassman, who joined me on a wellness retreat I embarked upon after my surgery, introduces the concept of "Eating Empowered" to emphasize nourishing the mind and body through informed food choice. It's a philosophy not about restricting one's diet but rather embracing a balanced, sustainable lifestyle that promotes overall health.

At its core, "Eating Empowered" is about fueling oneself with nutrient-dense foods that support both physical health and mental clarity. It encourages individuals to listen to their bodies, understand their unique nutritional needs, and make choices that align with their health goals. This approach moves away from fad diets and instead focuses on sustainable habits that can be maintained long-term.

A healthy gut plays a central role in achieving overall well-being, influencing everything from digestion to immune function and mood regulation.[27] The relationship between supplements, nutrition, and gut health is complex but crucial, because what we eat and the supplements we take can directly impact the balance of microorganisms in the gut (the microbiome). In turn, this affects our health and overall well-being. It is also increasingly recognized that anti-inflammatory nutrients and antioxidants play a pivotal role in maintaining gut health. Both types of compounds help manage inflammation and oxidative stress, which are key factors in gut-related disorders and diseases.

In incorporating the approach of Keri and Nutritious Life, in addition to other outside research, let's first look at anti-inflammatory nutrients, from reducing inflammation and oxidative stress to improving immune function and longevity. The tiny but powerful chemicals found in plant foods include foods rich in omega-3 fatty acids, turmeric, ginger, blueberries, pecans, artichokes, kidney beans, beets, cacao, cinnamon, red cabbage, green apples, green tea, sweet potatoes, and rosemary. The nutrients found in these foods help regulate the immune response and reduce chronic inflammation in the gut, which is crucial for preventing conditions like irritable bowel syndrome (IBS), inflammatory bowel disease (IBD), and other gastrointestinal issues.[28] Chronic gut inflammation can damage the intestinal lining, disrupt the balance of gut microbiota, and contribute to systemic health problems.

On the other hand, antioxidants protect the gut from oxidative stress, which occurs when free radicals (highly reactive and unstable molecules that can be made after exposure to toxins) cause cellular damage. Oxidative stress in the gut is linked to gut dysbiosis (microbial imbalance), leaky gut syndrome, and the development of chronic diseases. Key antioxidants like vitamin C (found in citrus fruits, bell peppers, and leafy greens), vitamin E, polyphenols, and flavonoids help neutralize free radicals and protect the gut lining from damage.[29] Polyphenols are plant-derived compounds found in a variety of fruits, vegetables, and beverages like green tea. They have also been shown to exert antioxidant properties in addition to anti-inflammatory effects. They help reduce oxidative damage in the gut and improve the health of the microbiome by promoting the growth of beneficial bacteria, which can further protect against inflammation and disease.

By reducing inflammation and oxidative stress, these nutrients from how we eat or the supplements we take can help maintain the integrity of the gut lining, support a balanced microbiome, and protect against gut-related diseases. Consuming a diet rich in omega-3 fatty acids, polyphenols, vitamins, and other antioxidants can be a powerful strategy for maintaining a healthy gut and preventing chronic conditions. Holistically, by making deliberate food choices, we can pursue healthier lifestyles. Of course, speak to your doctor or nutritionist for more personalized recommendations!

The Power of Protein

"Eating adequate protein helps your nervous system regulate."

Studies highlight that plant-based proteins (such as legumes, nuts, seeds, and grains) and phytochemicals (biologically active compounds found in plants) promote brain health. As a result, proteins play a crucial role in the functioning of the central nervous system (CNS), influencing everything from the formation and maintenance of neural structures to the transmission of signals across neurons. The CNS relies on proteins for a variety of vital functions, including neurotransmitter synthesis, synaptic signaling, cellular repair, and plasticity.

Why is this important? Proteins are directly involved in the synthesis, storage, and release of neurotransmitters, which are chemical messengers that transmit signals between neurons. Proteins also play a key role in supporting neuronal growth, survival, and synaptic plasticity, influencing cognitive functions like how we learn and our memory.[30] They are also essential for maintaining the structural integrity of neurons and the connections between them. Proteins not only contribute structurally and functionally but also participate in signaling pathways, apoptosis regulation, and stress responses. Just as important, they play a pivotal role in the prevention and treatment of neurodegenerative diseases.

Medicinal plants found in India also contribute significantly to neuroprotection. These plants, often rich in proteins and bioactive compounds, show promise in combating neurotoxicity.[31] Ashwagandha is commonly used for anxiety, fatigue, and neurodegenerative disorders, a powerful adaptogen that is known for enhancing stress resilience, improving memory and cognitive function, and supporting hormonal balance. And probiotics, which are a source of proteins and metabolites, have been identified for their role in regenerating myelin and enhancing neuronal communication, offering a novel pathway to combat neurodegeneration.

Saunas and Cold Plunges to Offset States of Chronic Stress

"We chase disease versus preventative care."

—Somi Javaid, MD, Founder of HerMD

In the modern wellness landscape, the trend for saunas and cold plunges is gaining popularity. Both are ancient therapeutic practices to counteract the adverse effects of chronic stress. Their physiological and psychological benefits stem from hormesis, a concept where controlled stressors elicit adaptive responses, strengthening the body's resilience.

Saunas harness the power of heat, exposing the body to temperatures typically ranging between 70°C and 100°C (158°F and 212°F). This induces a controlled, temporary stress response known as heat stress, which activates the hypothalamic-pituitary-adrenal (HPA) axis. A key component of this response is the release of heat shock proteins (HSPs), which play a vital role in cellular repair, enhancing protein stability, and boosting overall resilience. The heat exposure also triggers the sympathetic nervous system, prompting the release of norepinephrine—a neurotransmitter that sharpens focus, elevates mood, and combats inflammation. Regular sauna use has been linked to reduced markers of systemic inflammation, such as C-reactive protein (also known as CRP), and improved cardiovascular health, as demonstrated in research by Laukkanen and Laukkanen.[32] Moreover, saunas stimulate the release of endorphins, the body's natural "feel-good" chemicals, promoting relaxation and alleviating physical manifestations of stress. This makes saunas a potent tool for improving the body's ability to adapt to chronic stressors and building resilience over time.

On the opposing end of the spectrum, cold plunges or cryotherapy involve immersion in water temperatures below 15°C (59°F), usually for short increments. Immersion in water at these temperatures activates the sympathetic nervous system, leading to a dramatic increase in norepinephrine levels. This surge provides anti-inflammatory benefits, aiding in stress management.[33] Additionally, cold exposure stimulates the production of brown adipose tissue (also known as BAT), a type of fat that enhances metabolic efficiency and energy expenditure. This metabolic activation helps counteract stress-related physiological effects and can help to mitigate the physiological effects of stress, as well as to reduce cortisol levels, or cortisol recalibration.

Alternating between saunas and cold plunges combines the benefits of both by unlocking their synergistic capabilities. The rapid vasodilation induced by heat followed by vasoconstriction during cold exposure enhances circulation and promotes lymphatic drainage.

As a practice, these can both serve as a preventive approach to care—improving mood, helping emotional equilibrium, and enhancing endorphin release while reducing the stress hormone cortisol. Regular use has been associated with improved mental clarity, reduced symptoms of anxiety and depression, and an overall sense of relaxation. It can also elicit a focused presence and mindfulness practice as the intense sensory experiences demand focus, drawing individuals away from stress-inducing rumination.

Sex, Dopamine, and the Brain

When you orgasm, your brain releases a surge of dopamine. But when you have vaginal atrophy—which can occur during perimenopause and menopause—sex is no longer pleasurable, and sexual wellness becomes an added challenge.

Very few things can feel more deeply personal and vulnerable than our feelings about our sexual self. And sexual wellness—a vital aspect of human health—encompasses more than just the physical act of sex; it reflects our physical, emotional, and social well-being in relation to our sexuality. It correlates to our self-image, our perception of self-worth, our self-comfort, and our confidence. Balancing our relationship with estrogen and stress, perimenopause or menopause, and our decline in libido on top of vaginal dryness due to changes in hormones, the lack of desire post-childbirth can feel like a compounding downer—a downer absent of those natural dopamine "fixes."

Dr. Somi Javaid is a board-certified ob-gyn, a leading women's sexual health and menopause advocate, and the founder of HerMD, and dopamine and sexual wellness is what she would call her "sweet spot." Her insights emphasize the critical importance of addressing sexual wellness as an integral component of overall health.

She underscores that sexual wellness significantly influences various aspects of a woman's life, including mental well-being, confidence, relationships, and even vital signs like heart rate and blood pressure. She asserts that a healthy sex life is not merely a lifestyle choice but a vital indicator of overall health. Neglecting sexual health can lead to broader health implications, affecting both physical and emotional well-being.

Looking at sexual wellness, we see it is closely tied to emotional and psychological health. This is linked to the release of dopamine, endorphins, and oxytocin that occur during sexual activity, contributing to feelings of happiness, reduced stress, and enhanced emotional bonding with a partner. Oxytocin, often called the "love hormone," is particularly beneficial for fostering trust and emotional intimacy, which can mitigate feelings of loneliness and depression. Regular sexual activity has been shown to bolster the immune system, with sexually active individuals linked to having higher levels of immunoglobulin A (IgA), a critical antibody that plays a key role in immune defense. And sexual activity can act as a natural analgesic. The release of endorphins during sex reduces the perception of pain, making it a potential therapeutic intervention for conditions such as migraines and chronic pain syndromes.[34]

So, when sexual wellness is a cornerstone of our health, mentally and physically, how can we destigmatize conversations about this and find ways to bring comfortable and pleasurable, dopamine-releasing activities back into our everyday life?

Breaking down taboos is key to navigating feelings of discomfort and rediscovering enjoyable, dopamine-boosting experiences in our daily lives. With sexual function encompassing a wide spectrum—including desire, arousal, lubrication, orgasm, satisfaction, and pain—taking charge can feel daunting.

Here are some ways we can take charge, embrace vulnerability, and potentially feel less overwhelmed:

- Understand that *many* women are going through what you are.
- Embrace the framing of empowerment through community.
- Find ways to have open dialogue with your partner.
- Speak to specialists who are dedicating to finding solutions you can implement.
- Acknowledge there is more than one kind of desire.
- Debunk the belief that once you lose sexual desire it is gone forever.

Understanding stress and its impact on the body is complex and multifaceted. Stress is more than just a buzzword; it's a deeply intricate dance between our minds, our bodies, and our environments. It's the fight-or-flight instinct, the way we process life's demands, and for women, the ebb and flow of hormones across a lifetime. **But here's the thing: Stress doesn't have to control the narrative**. The more we understand it, the more we can pivot and take back the reins. We can rethink how we spend our precious time, reimagine what deserves our focus, and choose—deliberately—to fill our lives with what truly nurtures our mental and physical well-being. We can learn to nourish and nurture ourselves through understanding our positive stresses that energize us, versus the negative ones that deplete us, give grace to the hormonal fluctuations we naturally undergo, and take proactive ownership of our fitness routines, nutrition, and natural ways to alleviate chronic stress.

Together, step by step, we can shift from surviving to thriving.

Chapter 2 Contributors:

Sarah Kugelman, Tai Beauchamp, Melissa Guerrero, Stacy Igel Kavita Persaud, Sally Mueller, Somi Javaid, Marlyn Ortiz, Meg Hainer, Keri Glassman

3

The Evolved Meaning of Beautification

Redefining Self-Care and Self-Love as Acts of Empowerment

We can't think about pivoting to our best self from one dimension. In Chapter 2, we delved into the intricate connection between mental wellness, stress, and the physical toll it can take on our bodies. Now it's time to expand that conversation to include the love and respect we need to show ourselves—from head to toe, inside and out. It's about how we feel about how we look and recognizing the harmony between the two.

> "Mom, I am really mad at your body for what it did to you, but I am also proud of it for how hard it fought for you."
>
> **—My then-eight-and-a-half-year-old daughter when I arrived home after hospitalization**

In that moment—raw and unfiltered from a child—I realized something profound. Through her eyes, I recognized the quiet heroism of my body. Every day, it fights for me, even when I don't always fight for it. For many of us, we often get lost in the mirror, hyper-focused on every perceived imperfection—height, hair, skin tone, muscle definition, and a thousand other details. In today's world of social media filters and the booming accessibility of beauty treatments, the pressure to look perfect can feel suffocating.

But what if beauty wasn't about perfection? What if, instead of criticizing ourselves, we became our own fiercest allies? What if that scar—a permanent reminder of a 10-inch battle fought across my stomach—wasn't a flaw, but a badge of resilience? Instead of thinking, "I can never wear a two-piece again," I could say, "This scar is my story, and it's beautiful because I survived and came out stronger on the other side."

In this chapter, we'll challenge the notion of beauty as dictated by societal norms. Through the voices of women who've faced physical challenges, we'll explore self-acceptance, redefining body image perceptions, and celebrating the extraordinary power of our bodies. Together, we'll take the step to unlearn the conditioning that binds us and reclaim the freedom to define beauty on our terms, as our own best friends—not our harshest critics.

When Does Self-Criticism Begin?

Self-criticism about our physical attributes is like a quiet devilish companion, present in fleeting glances at the mirror or in the endless comparison to others on what we associate as a screen of perfection. It's the internal dialogue we have with ourselves that questions whether we're too tall, too short, too thin, or too thick; the voice that obsesses over scars, wrinkles, or any imperfections in our skin. Over time this becomes about more than just vanity—it becomes a deeply ingrained (bad) habit, nurtured by societal standards that tell us our worth is tied to how we look.

In an exploration of the question I just posed, let's flash to a dinner series I attended at Reyna, the delicious Mediterranean tapas restaurant in New York City. Called "Deconstructing Beauty," the dinner was co-hosted by life coach and author of *The Face of Anxiety* Trish Barillas, photographer and author Jamie Schofield Riva, and Motif beauty founder Devanshi Garg. Women from diverse career paths, with ages ranging from mid-20s to just under 50, were invited to attend. Everyone was dressed in chic attire, with each person's unique beauty radiating in their own way. Once cocktails were served and everyone was seated and given notepads and pens, Trish asked the group to start with this question: "When was the first time you started judging yourself about how you look?" Women paused, reflected, and then one by one started writing down their answers. After about 10 minutes of self-reflection, the sharing began: "*When someone told me my smile wasn't beautiful enough.*" "*When I was made fun off for wearing my hair up because my ears stick out.*" "*When I was told I was too tall.*" "*When I was told . . .*" and so on. It was a collective moment not just of reflection, but of realization that all of our individual self-judgment began because of outside perspectives and criticisms that passed judgment on us. It was an insightful recognition of the poignant notion that our inner critic often doesn't speak our truth, but rather echoes external expectations we've absorbed over our lifetime.

While this collective realization was a somewhat cathartic and a freeing moment that we all simultaneously shared, beyond our isolated dinner experience studies have confirmed the notion that self-criticism is deeply tied to a "social mirror," which is a habit where individuals evaluate their worth based on how they believe others perceive them.[1] This external pressure is increasingly detrimental in environments saturated with idealized body images propagated by media and social platforms.[2] And the internalized shame and self-criticism resulting from these comparisons eat away at us over time, fostering negative self-image and emotional distress. The associated psychological toll of this externalized self-criticism is significant, often linked to depression, anxiety, and reduced self-compassion.

As we sat together at our dinner, with our aha moment ripe as could be, we then pivoted to a conversation about how we at the table all saw each other—mostly women who were otherwise strangers, having met for the first time at this intimate setting. This was facilitated by the second exercise of the evening, where each woman was handed a card with another woman's photo on it and each of us was asked to mark the card with what we saw in that woman and answer the question "Beauty is . . ." Women noticed each other's attributes such as glowing skin, prominent cheekbones, thick eye brows, bountiful hair. The dialogue about the perception of beauty turned out to be quite the contrary of what many of us had been conditioned to believe about ourselves. What everyone saw in each other was beauty and admiration—complete strangers who saw the beauty in each woman across from them.

As our first chapter exercise, here's how you can try this exercise and experience the power of it at your next dinner party or girls' night out:

- Create a postcard of each guest.
- Add a photo of their choice to the postcard.
- Distribute the postcards.
- Give each guest a pen or pencil to highlight each woman's admirable attributes.
- Encourage each guest to add a "why" to the areas they highlight.
- Allow each guest to share the attributes of beauty they found in the women they wrote about.

Living with Anxiety, Body Image, and Self-Judgment

From the ages of 12 to 16, Jamie Schofield Riva, author of *Girlhood: Lost and Found*, who co-guided guests during the dinner at Reyna, faced a battle most would not know she had. Diagnosed with severe scoliosis, she spent four years confined to a back brace in an effort to avoid an invasive spinal fusing surgery. She wore big baggy clothes "to hide what was going on underneath." For Jamie, it wasn't just a brace; it was a cage, and she lived 1,460 days with her body trapped and suffocating in hiding. She battled the feeling of living with a body that betrayed her and was punishing her during her most formative years of childhood into adulthood, years when most girls are discovering who they are.

While the memories are vivid when she shares her story, she recognizes that it wasn't until she dove into photography and authorship that she truly realized the psychological impact this period of her life had on her self-image and self-confidence. If you met Jamie today, you would unequivocally see a tall, radiant woman, with long beautiful hair, a welcoming smile, and a presence that exudes self-assurance. But from age 12 onward she struggled with the idea of being beautiful or being "normal." She struggled with body image and self-worth issues stemming from the traumatic experience of her body being held hostage for four years, an experience that affected her self-perception and left her feeling like a monster.

In my interviews, countless women shared stories that illuminated this complex relationship—women born with health complexities that would shape a mindset they would eventually work to overcome, like Jamie, or like Kristy Rotonde, a thriving entrepreneur and founder of Plush Blow Dry Bars, who was born with a heart defect that brought unique challenges to her self-image due to two open heart surgeries. Think of the many women who are battling or have battled breast cancer, undergoing invasive procedures that result in scars that can lead to self-deprecation and debilitating insecurities. It cannot go without saying or be underestimated the journey of women who undergo invasive surgeries, such as mastectomies, and just how much they significantly impact a woman's self-confidence and body image. And while intellectually these procedures are lifesaving, they come with emotional and psychological burdens as women navigate changes in their physical appearance, sense of femininity, and self-worth.

> "The loss of a breast—a symbol often associated with femininity and motherhood—can lead to feelings of inadequacy and diminished sexual confidence. It's physically painful and mentally challenging in terms of self-image and self-worth and just feeling sexy."
>
> **—Dr. Meg Hainer, ob-gyn, and cancer survivor in remission**

> "I couldn't even have kids, and they are taking away my uterus because I have cancer, how fucking perverse is that?"
>
> **—Cate Luzio, founder and CEO of Luminary**

Also too common for many women, having a hysterectomy—particularly at a younger age—deeply influences a woman's perception of her body and sexuality. The removal of reproductive organs ties to a perceived loss of womanhood and can amplify feelings of isolation or depression. These outcomes are frequently compounded by societal stigmas and a lack of open discourse surrounding these surgeries.

These feelings are not isolated but pervasive; they reflect a universal truth about the mental weight we place on appearance. This weight ties closely to themes explored in Chapter 2, where we examined the interplay of stress and the body. How we feel internally and how we perceive ourselves externally are deeply interconnected, forming a feedback loop that can either nurture or hinder our confidence and sense of self.

By understanding this connection, we can begin to unpack and redefine what beauty means—not as perfection, but as a celebration of our stories, our resilience, and our individuality. It's not about erasing the scars but embracing the strength they symbolize.

A Journey of Unlearning: Breaking Free of Self-Judgment and Empowerment

> "The more successful women are, the more they need to reconcile loving themselves and have less fixation on physical perfection. Physicality occupies the front space of our brain, and it keeps us 'chained,' even though we are so accomplished."
>
> **—Stacey Widlitz, president of SW Retail Advisors and former CNBC retail analyst**

In a world that often prioritizes appearances, the greatest transformation comes when we learn to see ourselves with compassion and strength. When you undergo a wakeup call in life, two things happen—one, it scares the shit out of you, and two, it can redefine your mindset.

I often criticized my physical attributes because of exterior judgments that impacted my mindset toward what I believed was beautiful about me and what wasn't. Now in my upper 40s, I have had my stomach opened twice. Once was horizontally for an emergency C-section when my daughter was tangled in her umbilical cord two ways, causing her heart rate to drop with my every push and meaning she was not coming out otherwise. And once was vertically in order to untwist my intestinal obstruction before I went into life-threatening septic shock. Moments like these show us—powerfully—that our worth lies far beyond external appearances. These experiences taught me to see my body not as flawed, but as resilient, and my sense of worth shifted from external validation to inner strength. Such transformative experiences compel us to reevaluate what truly defines beauty and strength, leading to a shift in focus from external appearances to inner resilience, prompting a deeper, more meaningful relationship with ourselves. We learn that what matters is not the reflection in the mirror, but the resilience, grace, and determination that helps us endure life's most challenging moments.

The Power of Perspective

> "I need to honor and celebrate my body."
>
> **—Jamie Schofield Riva**

Jamie's story in this chapter is one of resilience and transformation. Her teenage years in the brace left scars that ran deeper than the physical, but they also fueled a journey of self-discovery. Through her photography and words, she has found healing and a reclaimed power—proving that even when our bodies seem to fail us, we can find strength in embracing our imperfections and redefining our narratives.

External influences shape all of us. However, life grants us pivotal moments to reshape our mindset and redefine our path. For some, the birth of a child or becoming a caretaker sparks this shift—a realization of our duty to model positivity and resilience for another generation. For others, it is a medical emergency or a personal crisis that stops the world in its tracks, urging us to acknowledge our mortality and find grace in imperfection.

Each of these experiences brings clarity: Our outward appearances pale in comparison to the depth of our character and the power of self-love. These moments, though difficult, hold the potential to liberate us from self-judgment and redefine what it means to truly live.

The Role of Self-Compassion

Fostering self-compassion and challenging these internalized beliefs can help mitigate the harmful effects of societal pressures. Practicing self-compassion allows us to break free from the cycle of self-criticism, enabling us to focus on our inherent worth rather than external judgments. Coming to a place where we can have a gentler lens with ourself, like you would a best friend, can have a positive impact not just on your self-confidence but your mental well-being.

Shifting your mindset toward a place of self-compassion can also positively impact your mental, emotional, and physical being as well, and help you unlock your stronger self. Studies[3] also suggest that the kinder we are to ourselves, the more we tame the feelings of depression, anxiety, and chronic pain.[4] It also suggests that individuals who are kinder to and more complementary of themselves tend to be more motivated to succeed at the things they wish to achieve because they are more likely to believe "I can."[5]

With a mindset of self-compassion and self-celebration, we can undergo a cognitive restructuring.[6] Organically, our minds are wired in a flight-or-fight mode, and that applies to our association with physical beauty as well. Someone insults us and we store that with a much heavier weight than a compliment, and this propels us into a sense of self-judgment and criticism. Self-criticism is often associated as a motivator in a flight-or-fight response, but what we need to give more weight to is the more impactful, positive opportunity of self-compassion and love.

Here are a few ways to transform self-loathing to self-love:

- **Focus on positive messaging.** Write down all your self-critical statements and then reframe each one as if you were speaking to a child—a child you wanted to uplift and give encouragement to.

- **Curate your social media.** Follow accounts that uplift and inspire you, and remove those that feed negativity.
- **Practice gratitude for your body.** Celebrate what your body can do—whether it's healing, nurturing, or simply carrying you through each day.
- **Focus on small wins.** Document moments where you overcame challenges, reinforcing the idea that you are stronger than you think.
- **Write yourself love notes.** Find sticky notes with statements, affirmations, or compliments and read them out loud to yourself.

When we choose to honor our bodies and our journeys, we redefine beauty—not as perfection, but as the strength and grace born from our struggles. This shift liberates us from self-doubt and invites us to embrace ourselves fully, with love and compassion.

Your Body as Story of Resilience: Embracing Aging, Personal Truth, and Natural Beauty

"As I began aging, I felt like I was preparing myself for battle."

—Jamie Schofield Riva

Doing the work of loving ourselves is an ongoing commitment, and it takes an ever-changing mindset. If we have challenges loving our young, youthful selves, then we must be ready to embrace the mindset that as we age, beauty evolves.

We get laugh lines, frown lines, scars from life events, wrinkles, skin that sags, stretch marks, all the things. When we look at nature, we see textures and lines and coloration, and we associate that with history and beauty. But when we look at ourselves, we have an unhealthy conditioning to associate any line or crack with imperfection rather than what it should be: a victory lap, a memory of achievement and milestones, a celebration of a marathon run, a child born, nights of endless laughter.

Aging is often viewed through the lens of loss—of youth, beauty, and vitality. Yet as we journey through life, the process of aging reveals a deeper narrative: one of transformation, authenticity, and self-discovery. Embracing aging means celebrating the natural beauty that accompanies each chapter of life and finding empowerment in our evolving personal truths.

Aging is not merely a physical change—it is a testament to resilience, growth, and experience. What if we think that as we age, our bodies and faces tell stories of laughter, perseverance, and wisdom, making the celebration of natural beauty all the more meaningful.

Historically, beauty standards have primarily emphasized youthfulness, leading to societal pressures that promote anti-aging products and procedures. However, a paradigm shift is emerging as more individuals and brands are championing the idea of "graceful aging"—like All Golden and Womaness mentioned in Chapter 2. Emerging cultural movements are also emphasizing a redefinition of beauty—one that embraces imperfection and authenticity. For instance, studies show that middle-aged and older women in urban China are redefining bodily aesthetics by balancing traditional values and modern ideals of fitness and grace. According to studies,[7] there is also a marked growing cultural movement that is reconnecting beauty with authenticity, self-care, and well-being. Similarly, the concept of "graceful aging" is reshaping how we approach physical changes, and we are slowly seeing wrinkles and gray hair being embraced as symbols of wisdom and vitality rather than flaws to conceal.[8]

This shift is redefining allure as something deeply tied to one's health, confidence, and natural self rather than just adhering to unattainable physical ideals. Embracing aging is as much an emotional journey as it is a physical one. In a world increasingly focused on youth and perfection, embracing the natural process of aging is an act of empowerment. The natural changes that accompany aging—lines that trace laughter, silver strands that glimmer with experience—are physical manifestations of a life lived with purpose, which is a topic we will delve into more deeply in the next chapter.

The voice of the inner critic is not a reflection of personal truth but an echo of external influences that have shaped our perceptions. Recognizing and challenging this voice is a critical step toward self-acceptance and mental well-being. From medically induced traumas to the perception of beauty via external pressures, we can slowly begin to choose our own definitions of what is beautiful for us and individuals. We can challenge who told us what beauty is and why we hold that as truth. We can pivot our mindset and embrace body gratitude at all stages of life, we can regularly acknowledge what our body has endured and accomplished, and celebrate that and find joy in who we are fully.

Chapter 3 Contributors:

Jamie Schofield Riva, Trish Barillas, Kristy Rotonde, Meg Hainer, Cate Luzio, Stacey Widltiz

4

Reprioritization: The Purpose Pivot Begins

Aligning Your Values and Time with Your Purpose

"I am in my soft era"

—Atoya Burleson, founder of Ladies Playbook and *insideLINES* podcast

Reprioritization is the transformative process of shifting focus from external pressures, societal expectations, or external validation toward internal clarity and personal fulfillment. It involves consciously redefining what truly matters based on our unique hierarchy of needs, aligning our decisions and actions with what brings peace, purpose, and balance. Success isn't a one-size-fits-all answer, and letting go of external pressure and finding peace in our own hierarchy of needs can be extremely empowering. Many times I have been on panels with highly successful women where we are asked, "How do you have it all?" One of the best responses I have heard (because it was so honest) was by Amy Shecter, then CEO of cosmetic dermatology services company Ever/Body: "You won't have it all." The fact is, "having it all" does not and should not mean the same thing to every single person. Instead, it comes down to taking the time to be retrospective and to think about what it means to us as individuals and letting that be our personal North Star in guiding our choices day to day, week to week, month to month.

In the first three chapters, we explored trusting our gut and the power of intuition, understanding the science of stress and its impact on our mental and physical being, and unraveling societal pressures associated with our external appearances. Now it's time to roll up our sleeves and begin the work of making space—making more space for the things that fuel us and making less space for what doesn't serve us.

At its core, reprioritization is about letting go of external pressures, which often manifest as obligations or benchmarks imposed by culture, work environments, or peers, leading to a life dictated by "shoulds" rather than our authentic desires. When we relinquish this weight, we free ourselves to explore what truly nourishes our mental, emotional, and physical well-being. When we look at how to get started in terms of prioritization, we often think of Maslow's hierarchy of needs: physiological safety, love/belonging, esteem, and self-actualization,[1] but it's in our self-actualization discovery that we begin to understand how we as individuals need to be loved, what it means to belong, what makes us feel safe, what drives our self-esteem.

In this chapter we will explore the work of self-discovery, our roadmap to finding our individual purpose, manifesting it, and balancing between achieving and maintaining both growth and letting go of the things that don't best serve us along the way.

The Work of Self-Discovery

> "People don't decide their futures; they decide their habits and their habits decide their future."
>
> —**F. M. Alexander**

It's human nature to be seduced, to be self-critical, to feel unsuccessful with where we are, especially in today's social media reel age. We see the perfect images, the idyllic vacations, and the seemingly flawless lives that flood our feeds, and if we stay on long enough we can become bombarded by a reel of envy. Because it's also human nature to crave what we don't have, or as Maslow would refer to it, "motivated by deficiency,"[2] we can often be triggered by a lack or perceived absence of something we momentarily believe to be essential in our lives. This leads to behaviors aimed at correcting perceived gaps in our life, which can manifest as anxiety, dissatisfaction, or an unhealthy striving for achievement.

But reality is: Feeling inadequate in comparison to these curated snapshots is just a trap. We start to believe that happiness and success are about what we lack—what we haven't achieved yet, what we don't possess. True happiness, however, isn't found in the analysis of what we don't have. Time and time again in my conversations, it has become clear that genuine happiness is about identifying what truly fulfills us as individuals. It's about understanding our own personal hierarchy of needs, which is likely different from each person around us, and embracing it. It's trusting that we all have a unique set of values, personal desires, and things that make us feel alive and bring us joy.

> "Life isn't a competition; it's an experience and an individualistic journey that keeps evolving."
>
> **—Melissa Guerrero, VP/DMM, cosmetics retail executive**

Melissa Guerrero, whom we first met in Chapter 2, has a story that is a testament to this truth. In her young forties, she faced a life-altering diagnosis: breast cancer. A wife, a mother of two, and a driven professional, she found herself confronting not only the physical challenges of chemotherapy and surgeries but also the emotional weight of possibly missing out on her children's lives. This unexpected pause in her career—forced by illness—became an unintentional gift. It allowed her to reevaluate what mattered most.

She began asking herself difficult but necessary questions: "I know what I'm grateful for, but am I truly enjoying those things? Am I living a life that aligns with my purpose? How can I make the time to pursue the things that matter most?"

Melissa's journey of self-discovery wasn't entirely unfamiliar. As a successful executive, she spent years refining strategies for growth and success in her professional life. What she hadn't realized, however, was that these same tools could be applied to her personal life. With intention and focus, she began leveraging the skills she'd mastered at work—goal-setting, prioritization, and reflection—to reconstruct a life centered on joy, purpose, and impact.

Through this process, Melissa uncovered what truly makes her thrive: helping others discover their strengths and grow. For her, fulfillment wasn't about chasing external markers of success but rather leaning into what ignites her spirit. In this purpose exploration she came to recognize that what makes her thrive is her ability to help people, help them find their strengths, and help them grow. Now with this adjusted lens, she is making more purposeful decisions and life choices that fulfill her in new ways.

Here is the first exercise in your work to self-discovery:

- When do you feel most alive? List five things that can get you up in the morning without an alarm clock.
- How are you making the time for these things?
- What beliefs might be holding you back from making the time, and how can you challenge those beliefs?
- List three ways you will hold yourself accountable for making the time.

What Is Growth Wisdom?

There are many avenues you can take toward self-discovery, and to get there you must have not only an open mindset but an always learning one. "Growth wisdom" refers to the insights and knowledge we gain through personal development, life experiences, and overcoming challenges. It emphasizes the importance of learning from both successes and failures to foster resilience, adaptability, and a deeper understanding of yourself and the world, and it often encompasses emotional intelligence, self-awareness, and the ability to reflect on past experiences to inform future decisions.

As leaders we often hear the term "growth mindset" and we are adept at applying that thought process to the job. It means we are willing to take risks, to experiment, and to challenge ourselves in order to grow and learn. It serves us well and feeds our determination to succeed.

But when we lean into this on a personal level, we go on a deeper journey. We open our minds to learn more about ourselves as individuals. We actively engage in an introspection that allows us to gain clarity about our values, our beliefs, and our motivations. **And here's the beautiful part**: As we uncover our hierarchy of needs, we also grow to learn over time that our hierarchy isn't static. It evolves as we grow. It evolves as we grow at home, as we grow professionally, and as we cultivate our friendships. For example, with life stages come different priorities. As a single professional we might value independence and achievement, while a new parent may prioritize nurturing their children over independence. These shifts are not contradictions but evolutions of our understanding of what matters to us most as individuals at different points in our lives.

In addition to an open mind, growth wisdom requires vulnerability. It requires the courage to admit when we're wrong, to acknowledge that we don't have all the answers, and to seek help when we need it.[3] It requires a level of self-awareness and the ability to recognize our triggers and the obstacles that prevent our growth. These moments of humility teach us resilience and open us to learning throughout of lives.

Growth wisdom is not a destination; it's a lifelong journey.[4] It's the voice that reminds us to be kind and patient when we think we're falling short of our own expectations, to pause and reflect on what each life moment is teaching us and to embrace the opportunities to learn. The more attuned we become with listening to our individual needs, the more the external noise quiets, and this allows us to find confidence in trusting we know what fills our cup. It also empowers our self-trust and over time enables us to embrace our intuition and trust that the path we are carving for ourselves is the path we belong on. And importantly, it allows us to give ourselves grace, because we realize that evolving priorities don't mean abandoning past values—they reflect growth and a deeper understanding of ourselves (something we will further explore in Chapter 6).

Exploring the Natural Tensions

Life is a constant dance between stability and exploration, two forces that often pull us in opposing directions, yet shape the essence of a fulfilling existence. Stability offers us security and comfort, a foundation where we feel safe. Exploration, on the other hand, propels us into the unknown, fostering excitement and growth. These forces—grounding and adventure—are the natural tensions that shape our paths.

Let's first look at the elements of life that give us our grounding, help us feel safe, bring us consistency, and bring us comfort in that stability. Stability is the bedrock of our lives, the place we return to when the world feels chaotic or overwhelming. It manifests in our daily routines, our intimate relationships, and the rituals we depend on to give us peace—like that first cup of coffee or morning walk with your dog. Maslow emphasized this foundational need in his hierarchy of needs, where safety and security are positioned as prerequisites to higher levels of self-actualization.[5] Stability isn't just about physical safety; it's about emotional grounding—the people and habits that remind us of who we are when everything else feels uncertain.

But sometimes when we see people having experiences we haven't had or we learn of something we missed out on, that stability can start to feel less fulfilling. While stability grounds us, exploration fuels us. After all, while the human spirit craves stability, it also craves growth. And this is why when we experience something new, we feel energized. This can be anything from a new skill that gives us a sense of accomplishment or traveling to a new destination that allows us to discover and nourish our minds, and everything in between. In Chapter 2, we talked about the positive stress—eustress—that increases motivation and releases endorphins. That's what engaging in novel and challenging activities does for us.

When we look at the experiences that fuel our adventurous side, our discoveries, and our growth, the tension with our need for stability is often not in a steady equilibrium, because as we change, our needs and expectations change. It takes self-discovery to find what gives us the psychological safety zone we need while also feeling energized and fulfilled.

The challenge in growth and prioritization is navigating the tensions between these two forces, the forces of stability and of excitement. Overloading on stability can feel stagnating and unmotivating, while an overemphasis on constant adventure seeking can leave us feeling untethered and burned out. In our personal introspection we can begin to uncover what our ideal individual balance is.

For our second exercise in this chapter, here is your work:

Let's start with stability anchors:

- What routines make you feel grounded? Think about those elements in your life that provide grounding—your routines, your relationships, your safe spaces.
- Who in your life makes you feel understood?
- What spaces provide you with a sense of calm?

Second, think about what experiences ignite your adventurous spirit:

- What keeps you learning and growing?
- What gives you that positive stress, the stress that releases those positive endorphins?
- How do you define adventure?

Now, set a personal balance challenge:

- Choose one stabilizing activity and one adventurous activity to incorporate into your week.
- Reflect on how they made you feel.

What Is My Personality Index?

As we take an introspective evaluation, we can't fully access that assessment without also considering our personality index measurement. Our personality index is a tool that reveals insights about what motivates us, what energizes us, and what challenges us. Usually encountered during job interviews or professional team-building exercises, these evaluations are not just workplace tools; they are windows into our natural tendencies and behaviors. They can illuminate what drives us, what we naturally gravitate toward, and what we may shy away from. From the Myers-Briggs Type Indicator (MBTI), which explores how we perceive the world and make decisions, to the Predictive Index (PI), which examines our behavioral drives—like Dominance, Extraversion, Patience, and Formality—alongside cognitive abilities, to CliftonStrengths, which focuses on our innate talents and how to maximize them, these tools provide powerful frameworks for self-awareness and growth.

For example, per my own PI, I am annotated as a Captain, a profile that emerges when someone's behavioral pattern shows specific traits in terms of Dominance, Extraversion, Patience, and Formality—categorizing me as someone with high dominance and extraversion, with a preference to operate at a faster pace, eager to move on new ideas, and able to operate with less formality. And per My CliftonStrengths, I am a Futuristic, Strategic Activator and Achiever—which means I thrive on working hard, possess a great deal of stamina, take immense satisfaction in being busy and productive, can make things happen by turning thoughts into action, create alternative ways to proceed, am inspired by the future and what that could be, and feel confident in my ability to take risks. These assessments likely explain my drive to pursue new endeavors and my deep-seated resilience—a trait that also likely propelled me to write this book after a traumatic medical experience.

As we assemble and more deeply understand the puzzle pieces of who we are, what makes us tick, what makes us thrive, we find what gives us our energy. These questions also guide us toward understanding how to more powerfully align our strength with our goals. This self-awareness empowers us to release the false notion of believing that our happiness and fulfillment are dictated by that of others. And this evaluation gives us enlightenment toward discovering ourselves and our sense of purpose.

In my assessment of my personal hierarchy of needs, I have grown to let go of envy and allow others joy to be my joy for them. Through self-discovery we learn that we all have different needs, different tendencies, different affinities and aversions. We are in various life stages, have differing family dynamics, and varying responsibilities. As someone identified as a Futurist, I thrive on exploration and innovation. Balancing this aspect of myself with my roles as a wife and mother has required intentional effort. For example, while my professional travels sometimes pull me away from home, they also fuel my energy and creativity. By honoring this duality and making thoughtful compromises, I find balance—not by striving to "have it all" in the traditional sense, but by defining what "having it all" means for me personally.

> "It's not about balance; it's about accepting the inevitable tradeoffs, doing what you can, when you can and embracing the idea that sometimes 'balance' may not exist."
>
> **—Emma Grede, serial entrepreneur**

Achieving self-discovery is not a one-time event and this assessment doesn't come overnight. It's an ongoing process of trusting your inner needs as explored in Chapter 1 and embracing your unique path. It requires acknowledging that happiness and fulfillment are not finite resources. It encompasses the acceptance that just because someone else is experiencing something amazing that you are not, it doesn't diminish our own happiness, but instead it's an opportunity to expand and embrace the richness of our diverse experiences.

In that acceptance we find that fulfillment comes from understanding our priorities and embracing the journey we are currently on. This understanding brings us freedom. It unburdens us and allows us to focus on our own priorities, to celebrate our personal journey. And our fulfillment emerges not from ticking off a universal checklist of success but from deeply understanding who we are, what we need, and where we want to go.

The Roadmap to Finding Purpose

Digging deeper into reprioritizing and pivoting into our higher purpose, I reflect on the story of Jill Katz, founder of Assemble HR Consulting.

With a 13-week-old baby and a daughter just a few years older, Jill had an experience that catapulted her journey to finding her individual purpose. It began during a visit to family in Boston during Thanksgiving weekend in 2009. During her stay, she experienced a sudden and unexpected weakness, which she initially attributed to overeating, when she found herself unable even to walk on a treadmill. Despite this "random" incident, which she wrote off as "an odd occurrence," she enjoyed the Thanksgiving weekend and drove home to New Jersey that Sunday. Upon returning, she noticed that she was still experiencing weakness and fatigue, which she further attributed to stress and exhaustion.

Jill had just returned to work after having a baby and was experiencing stress from her new job and from motherhood. Initially, she dismissed her symptoms as a panic attack, but her husband insisted they visit a doctor after she found herself walking down a flight of stairs in her home not able to finish a sentence while on a call with a friend. Her initial reaction to his insistence was "But I have dinner plans tonight." He wasn't having it and called her doctor right away.

The doctor found Jill's oxygen levels to be extremely low and advised her to go to the emergency room. By the time she arrived at the hospital she couldn't speak at all. Reflecting back, she doesn't even remember the drive to the ER. She was quickly assessed and put on an IV, and a doctor later informed her that she was having a pulmonary embolism—a large blood clot blocking her left pulmonary artery—and six clots in her right lung. The doctor told her she had about two hours to live. Jill spent five nights in the cardiac ICU and was on blood thinners for 19 months. The experience left her traumatized, avoiding exercise that raises her heart rate out of fear of another embolism. Now 15 years later, she still takes blood thinners when flying or driving long distances.

Most importantly, this life-altering experience stopped Jill in her tracks on the realization that she pushed herself so hard that it could have meant she was no longer present in her son's and daughters' lives. It was a "holy shit" time, a newfound understanding of the importance of proactive health management, self-care, and balance. It led her to reevaluate everything, including how she worked—which led her to create a hybrid work environment in a time when that didn't widely exist in corporate culture—and ultimately to her leaving her career in 2018 to start her own business as a leadership development and strategy coach focused on helping others. Now best known for the #CandorCourageAndCare™ Feedback Model, she and her team help transform teams, find value in relationships, and unlock value through accountability and authentic ways.

When life stops us in our tracks, it's often a time that we search for our higher purpose as part of our path to recovery. But while the trauma triggers the exploration, there is still work ahead and it can feel daunting to achieve. Nancy Berger (whom we met in Chapter 1 and who has been battling her own major health issues for years) leaned into her awakening by reminding herself that "every day is a precious gift." For her this means leaning into things that fulfill her: being a connector, working on innovative projects that propel business into the next frontier, bringing people value. Jill found her higher purpose as both a mom of two and as an executive coach, dedicating herself to helping teams have more honest and productive relationships.

In my conversations with women who actively explored their personal filter to arrive at finding their sense of purpose and thus opening a mindset for what should be on their "important list,"[6] here are the things that stand out consistently:

- **Engage in self-reflection.** When we experience trauma or significant life changes, it can catapult us into self-reflection. While life events are often a catalyst, this exploration can begin at any time. In this we begin to assess our values, our passions, and our interests.
- **Be open to exploring new experiences.** When we are willing to engage in diverse activities, we discover what resonates within us.
- **Embrace challenges and the unknown.** Step out of your safe-zone and be open to facing challenges and learning from failures.
- **Build like-minded connections.** This was one of the most fulfilling factors as I researched and began to write this book. And by like-minded, I don't mean "like me," but rather finding a commonality of connection. In many of my conversations our commonality was a significant life event, medical moment, or mental evolution. And through sharing, in every call I had, we all learned.

- **Seek guidance.** This one was probably the least common, because as women we tend to try to "power through anything." But those who embraced seeking guidance as an asset (albeit through a therapist or coach) found tremendous success on their path to purpose.
- **Commit to always listening and learning.** Life events, accomplishments, setbacks, they all contribute to new sets of information and opportunities. As we stay open to that, open to the opportunities of new experiences, we continue to home in on our sense of purpose.

Just as we have differing hierarchy of needs, different factors fuel what satisfies our sense of purpose. The more introspective we are willing to be, the closer we come to trusting our inner voice, our experiences and can embrace our individual journeys. And if one commonality stood out in all my conversations with women it's that the desire to "live our purpose" is a synonymous factor to "feeling truly successful."

Our sense of purpose can be fueled by various factors and is a multifaceted construct influenced by personal motivations, social relationships, value systems, and life experiences. These are the intrinsic elements, and these are influenced by personal interest and enjoyment. This drives us to gravitate to and engage in activities that align with our values and passions to arrive at greater meaning in our lives. There is a natural desire to belong, and in our craving for strong social ties and supportive relationships, we gravitate to opportunities that enhance our sense of purpose by providing a framework for shared goals and values with others.

Putting Things on the Important List

> "You simply must believe that the source of your well-being and success is nothing other than the power of your own mind."
>
> **—Dr. James Doty, author of *MindMagic*[7]**

Now that we have taken a dive into the work of self-discovery and creating a roadmap to finding purpose, we can also refer back to the book's preface and Chapter 1, where we explored how the power of intention and manifesting can be an effective tool toward rewiring your brain. It's a tool primed to subconsciously seek out something you want or the steps you need to take to reach a certain goal. As you home in on your purpose and the things you want to prioritize, you also have the power to convince yourself it's within reach.

Based on research by top neuroscientist Dr. James Doty, one can change their mindset and, along the way, create and strengthen neural pathways that motivate the brain to make a dream or vision come true. He refers to this as "embedding your intention"—tying into the neuroscience of neuroplasticity and teaching your brain that certain things are most important—programming your brain to focus on turning what's important into your reality. This is how we form habits that allow us to grow into achieving our goals.

Here's how it works: when we repeat an action or thought pattern, our brain strengthens specific neural pathways, making the behavior or mindset habitual.[8]

According to Dr. Doty, to embed your intention, use as many sensory organs as possible:

- Write it down.
- Read it silently.
- Read it aloud.
- Visualize it.
- Make it salient; embed it into the subconscious.
- **Now it's on your brain's important list and your attention network is activated.**[9]

Engaging multiple senses simultaneously strengthens our memory and learning.[10] Writing our goals activates motor skills, reading them aloud engages auditory processing, and visualizing taps into the visual cortex—all working together to embed the intention more deeply. Additionally, as we work through what matters most to us, we find that goals are easier to prioritize and achieve when they carry deeper emotional significance. When a goal resonates emotionally, not just intellectually, it engages our limbic system, as studied by neuroscientist Antonio Damasio. This engagement amplifies our motivation and preservice to said goals. For example, while pursuing things for financial success satisfies a basic need of survival, understanding *the why our goals matter* and tying it to the ability to serve our higher purpose makes the goal more compelling, enhancing our commitment to achieving it.

Balancing Work and Personal Life as Women

> "Am I prioritizing deadlines over meaningful relationships? Am I chasing external validation at the cost of inner peace? Who am I beyond my work title or the company I represent?"

These are just a few of the many questions women, including myself, internalize and grapple with in our quest to balance the demands of work and personal life.

Whether we're early in our careers, navigating the challenges of new motherhood, or redefining priorities in the later stages of our professional journeys, the tightrope we walk often feels daunting and overwhelming. The weight of societal expectations and the self-imposed pressure to excel in all areas of life can be overwhelming. When we carry the myth of "having it all," it sets us up with impossible standards and fuels cycles of self-judgment and guilt.

The result? A constant tug-of-war between professional aspirations and personal obligations, leaving little room for rest or meaningful self-care. Many women struggle with feelings of inadequacy, believing they aren't doing enough for their families or falling short in their careers. In prioritizing others' needs, we often neglect our own mental and physical well-being.

But what if the balance we seek isn't about perfection? What if it's about discovering a harmony rooted in self-reflection, guided by purpose, and anchored in healthy reprioritization? What I have witnessed time and time again, is that as we find the harmony we also actually thrive to greater heights in our professional realms.

> "Through my journey, I learned the only thing you can't take back is time."
>
> **—Kristy Rotonde, founder of PlushBlow, blow-dry bars**

Kristy Rotonde, introduced in Chapter 3, is a mother, wife, and entrepreneur whose journey is an example of the power of self-reflection. She was born with Tetralogy of Fallot, a rare condition caused by a combination of four heart defects that are present at birth. Tetralogy of Fallot defects cause oxygen-poor blood to flow out of the heart and into the rest of the body and can cause viral illnesses. To protect her, she had her first open heart surgery, an experimental one, at age five, replacing her valve with one made out of clay. It led her to live a cautious life, one where she had to be careful around what felt like everything—careful at the pool because she would easily turn blue, careful at the park so she didn't fall, and so on. As a teenager she always felt "different" because of her big scar, which took an emotional toll on her self-confidence.

At age 34 she was told that her artificial valve was melting, causing her heart to be enlarged. She had to undergo another surgery or risk "not being here in a week." She had a panic attack, all while also going through a divorce that was forcing her to shut down her businesses. Post-surgery she felt like she woke up every day with "a lion behind her back," chasing her and not allowing her to find space and room to breathe. But as she got through her divorce, found a new love, recovered, and became a mom, she found a new peace she never knew.

"Work is no longer first above all." Through her physical journey, Kristy found mental and emotional clarity and balance. She began finding her alone time space daily, even if just for a walk or a 10-minute mediation. She embraces life's mortality and the importance of friends, family, herself, and her invaluable gift of the role of motherhood. She is finding comfort and happiness in being the best mom she can be, meaning self-care for herself first.

Self-reflection like Kristy's is the starting point for finding balance. And balance will never be a perfect, static place. It's ever evolving. It requires pausing and openly assessing what aspects of life deliver joy, bring us energy and fulfillment, and what drains our soul. Connecting with purpose can also help navigate the noise of external expectations and pressures. The work of our purpose journey acts as a compass, guiding our decisions about how to prioritize where to focus our attention and energy.

Building upon earlier exercises in this chapter around purpose and setting the important list, here are action steps to set intentional boundaries, with purpose as your North Star:

- What are the tasks or to-do's that serve your important list? Write them down.
- What tasks can you decline that align with your long-term goals, even if they seem urgent in the moment?
- Reflection: How have your lists surprised you, and what does that illustrate to you?

In this journey of reflection, remember that priorities shift over time. We see that as we embrace our growth wisdom. A woman in the early stages of her career may focus on professional growth, while later she might emphasize family or personal passions. Allowing for these shifts fosters grace and adaptability. Further, success doesn't have to mean excelling in every area of life simultaneously. Instead, it can mean being present in the moment, whether at work, with family, or during self-care. Understand that rest is not a luxury; it's a necessity. Taking breaks and setting aside time for self-care are acts of strength, not selfishness. And, importantly, replace self-critical thoughts with self-affirmations.[11] For example, instead of saying, "I'm failing at everything," say, "I'm doing my best in the moment, and that is enough."

The Balance Between Achieving and Maintaining Growth and Letting Go

> "Where am I negotiating with myself to say yes to some things and no to others?"
>
> **—Leila Hormozi, CEO of Acquisition.com[12]**

Leila Hormozi, host of *The Build with Leila Hormozi Podcast*, has a way of delivering fast, sharp insights that cut through the noise. I digest her insights regularly. In one episode, she said something that struck me deeply in terms of relevance to this section: "When we look at people like Mother Theresa or the Dalai Lama, they don't have more hours in a day than we do. But they spend each hour of their day doing things that matter, things of impact."

Her words felt like a spotlight, illuminating a question many of us avoid asking: How am I truly spending my time? Are the hours slipping through my fingers on things that drain me, or are they devoted to things that create meaning, growth, and impact?

This realization felt like a powerful invitation to pause and reflect. What would happen if we became more intentional with our time—releasing the distractions, letting go of the trivial, and dedicating ourselves to what truly matters? What if we gave ourselves permission to let go of what doesn't serve us in order to nurture the things that do?

The journey of self-discovery and purpose also provides a roadmap for achieving balance between growth and sacrifice. It's not just about growing—it's about maintaining that growth through intentional choices, deliberate delegation, and a clear-eyed focus on what leads to a life of impact.

> "You think there is an invisible weight on your shoulders at all times."
>
> **—Cate Luzio, founder and CEO, Luminary**

In 2023, Cate Luzio, founder and CEO of Luminary, faced one of the most defining moments of her life. Her relationship with her health shifted into hyperdrive as she navigated a life-changing battle with breast cancer, culminating in the need for a lumpectomy and later a hysterectomy. For two years during the pandemic, Cate had postponed her mammogram, caught in the determination and drive of building her business, always finding something else that took priority. Like many high-achieving women, she prided herself on and was driven by the belief that she had to do it all herself.

But everything changed when she took a test that would alter her perspective on life.

Cate founded Luminary in 2018 after leaving a successful two-decade career in banking. Her vision was to create a space where women—and allies—could come together to advance one another's careers. What began as an entrepreneurial mission grew into a global professional education and networking platform with thousands of members and hundreds of corporate partners. Today, Luminary hosts events, workshops, and structured programs designed to foster growth and connection. For Cate, the work was (and still is) deeply personal. She pours herself into it, often taking the stage to inspire and empower others. But one day, just as she was about to step onto that stage, a phone call from her doctor changed everything. Her mammogram results were in: a positive diagnosis for breast cancer.

Cate's life, once dictated by a relentless drive to do everything herself, took an abrupt turn. A dedicated entrepreneur who almost never took a day off, she was forced not just off the stage but offline completely. It was a humbling and transformative period, one that taught her a powerful lesson: she couldn't control everything.

As she went offline, she had to surrender herself to refocusing her priorities and letting go of the things she could, and frankly should, delegate to others. In her recovery, where she learned she didn't have to be on 24/7, she was forced into the practice of radical reprioritization. She realized how at the core of it, she had to learn how to accept help and support, and to trust. What she learned to embrace was that she built a great team, one that she could not only rely on but must be able to learn to trust. "Trust is hard for founders, but it is required," she reflects. And when one can trust and let go, they learn to shine a light on their own personal strengths that have been drowned out by trying to do "all the doing." The reality she learned was that none of us build greatness alone. In this Cate found power in her vulnerability. She was able to discover the gift in the support she had around her. She was able to see a team she built shine. She was able to reprioritize as she let go, not only focusing on her well-being, but as she recovered, on stepping into her highest powers for the company she was building. And in her ability to let go, she grew in new, profound ways.

Healthy Selfishness

I will end this chapter with this liberation: Making yourself a priority, delegating to others to create space, and making your own personal important list is a healthy practice.

For many of us, the word "selfish" is associated with an insult, implying neglecting others for personal gain. But what we can come to understand as we go through our of journey of self-discovery is that not all selfishness is harmful. In fact, there's a form of selfishness that's not only healthy but necessary for living a balanced, fulfilling life. This is what psychologists and wellness advocates call healthy selfishness—the ability to prioritize your own needs without guilt, understanding that taking care of yourself enables you to better care for others.[13]

Why does healthy selfishness matter? Because prioritizing ourselves in a healthy way reduces stress and anxiety. It also increases our ability to contribute more meaningfully to the areas we spend our time and energy. When we learn to say no (which we explore more in Chapter 7), and we set clear boundaries and replace guilt with self-compassion, we find empowerment and well-being through the space we make for ourselves.

Here are action steps to take to building balance and letting go:

- **Practice radical reprioritization.** Identify what truly matters in your life and career. Write down your top three priorities and focus on them for the next three months. Mark your calendar and note any differences in how your energy feels.
- **Delegate and trust.** Make a list of things others on your team are stronger at than you, then let them do those things and share progress updates.
- **Celebrate progress over perfection.** Build a milestone calendar, and acknowledge the wins. You will find a worksheet for this in the book's appendix.
- **Embrace vulnerability as a strength.** Trust that life is a continuous learning cycle. Focus on those learnings and experiences that reshape you.
- **Prioritize your health and wellness.** Remind yourself that taking care of your needs isn't selfish—it's the act of being responsible.

In the context of Maslow's hierarchy of needs, the work of self-discovery means reconnecting with foundational aspects like health, safety, and love, while allowing self-actualization to guide your long-term goals. By prioritizing personal growth over fleeting achievements, we create space to find balance and deeper fulfillment. Reprioritization, however, is not about abandoning responsibilities but reshaping them in ways that feel achievable and rewarding and help you fulfill your purpose.

Ultimately, reprioritization is a journey toward inner peace—a deliberate and ongoing effort to realign with what truly matters, fostering a life driven by inner harmony rather than external expectations. It's not about doing less but about doing what resonates most with your authentic self.

Chapter 4 Contributors:

Atoya Burleson, Mina Fader, Jill Katz, Nancy Berger, Kristy Rotonde, Cate Luzio, Amy Shecter, Jane Hanson, Emma Grede

5

The Things I Am Grateful for and Finding Grace

Cultivating Gratitude and Grace in Everyday Life

"In the world of dualities there is no end to perfection. But in the field of inner self there is no chance for imperfection!"

—**Gurudev Sri Sri Ravi Shankar**

GRATITUDE CAN ARISE from the most unexpected places. My list of things that I am grateful for post-surgery spans from the surface level to my inner being. I am grateful for elastic-waist pants (a revelation that has transformed my wardrobe); for jumpers and rompers, my instant mood boosters; and for strategically designed swimsuits, a marvel in the world of women's fashion that should have come to us all sooner. On the surface, as a woman who lived in skinny jeans, I have had to accept they may no longer be my best friend and that is okay, because an element I am even more grateful in my self-realization journey is knowing that I am far from alone in sometimes struggling to appreciate all the ways I can dress and feel good with a stomach that will never not have loose skin, a scar from above my belly button to my pubic bone, and the inevitable element of age. And more deeply beyond the surface, I am grateful for the ability to embrace the power of growth wisdom and for the journey I get to be on in writing this book, having the space for deeply engaging conversations with women I admire, and having the opportunity to give every women I speak with the space to tell their story and share the gift of their learnings and insights.

From our feelings about our bodies, our scars, our failures, and our triumphs, a positive mindset and maintaining positive expectations takes work. Once we embrace that recovery doesn't happen overnight, both physically and emotionally, we begin to realize that the journey itself can open other gifts we couldn't see or appreciate before.

I remember in my moment of shock being told I needed to make a choice about emergency surgery, the number one thought that flooded my mind was my daughter and my fear of all the moments I could miss in her life if I wasn't around. It scared the shit out of me. And that news was like a tidal wave hitting my entire being, putting my whole world into a new perspective. And as doctors told me, "it will be hard for you as a Type A person, but healing *will* take time and you will need to find patience," all I could think of was not letting only myself down but letting down the little girl who had the largest scare of her life through me. That fear became my inner mantra, pushing me forward to have the needed patience. And through my forced pause and healing process I found grace and a new gratitude perspective—grace for myself and gratitude for the unexpected gifts I am lucky enough to have been granted in the process.

Patience becomes a crucial ally during the healing journey. Rather than fixating on the end goal of full recovery, we learn to appreciate the small accomplishments along the way. For me this meant the first time I could walk unassisted, the first time I could eat a meal without completely cramping up, the first time I could take a shower (gosh that running water felt so good), and the first time the scale showed I weighed over 100 pounds again—just to name a few. In these small triumphs, we discover the power of gratitude. And we begin to offer ourselves kindness and grace, a realization that fuels an empowered mindset. Through tiny milestones and the larger lessons that they reveal, we learn just how much beauty there is in every stage of the journey.

As we navigate our purpose-driven journeys, we will encounter twists, turns, and revelations that shape us in ways we never expected. Through it all, gratitude and grace are essential companions. They help us embrace the lessons found in setbacks and celebrate the progress we often overlook.

In this chapter, we will explore inspiration from others—stories and reflections that remind us of the many ways gratitude can transform our perspective and illuminate unexpected gifts along the way.

Grateful for Trusting Self-Advocacy

> "I didn't want to feel weak, but I learned over time that sometimes a little bad may need to happen in order to ignite the good."
>
> **—Lolita Lopez, reporter, NBC4 News**

Diagnosed with breast cancer in 2013 after finding a tumor during an at-home self-exam, Lolita Lopez was well into her on-camera career as a news reporter. Feeling like her body had "hit a wall," she had trusted her instincts and performed a self-exam. When she felt the lump, she was sure that something wasn't right. The diagnosis she received meant undergoing a double mastectomy. In those initial days, Lolita grappled with a deep fear of appearing weak, and she worried about how others might perceive her pause from work to prioritize her health. She looked at her professional needs over her personal as a first reaction.

Her perspective was far from unique. Through my interviews of women who have faced medical challenges, physically or mentally, it is all too common that most individuals find themselves consumed by the fear of showing vulnerability and by the thought "I can't show weakness." But the reality is, this fear often masks a critical truth: These are pivotal moments in our lives that illustrate how strong we truly are.

Through her healing journey, Lolita has learned to let go of what no longer serves her, to speak up for her personal needs, and to make her health an uncompromising priority. Eleven years later, when she learned she would need to replace her implants, thus facing her second surgery and a procedure she knew would involve a difficult recovery, she approached it decisively. "As soon as I saw an available timeslot, I grabbed it. No stalling. No second guessing. I embraced the fact that work will be okay, I have a team and my health comes first. Period."

While a decade prior, there was an initial pause in how to address her medical condition, Lolita has a whole new relationship with herself, and this journey has redefined her relationship with self-care and self-advocacy. She is now even more acutely aware of her feelings, and when something is not right her reaction is to immediately listen to her body with unwavering attentiveness. She has learned to prioritize her feelings, trust what is uncomfortable, and acknowledge that those feelings are real and she gives herself permission to be proactive about self-advocacy.

An invaluable lesson in self-empowerment entails understanding the difference between being in power and being empowered. Empowerment isn't about controlling every situation but about owning our agency to act in ways that align with our well-being. And for many, it requires a shift in mindset—a willingness to honor our needs, advocate for ourselves, and recognize that asking for help or taking a pause is not a sign of weakness but an act of courage and care.

And being empowered and embracing self-advocacy is more than a skill; it's a vital component of living a life that recognizes our needs and allows us to make choices that align with our priorities. By trusting ourselves, seeking support when necessary, and prioritizing self-care, we not only empower ourselves but also inspire others to do the same. In a world that often celebrates unrelenting strength and productivity, it's important to remember that true strength lies in the ability to pause, reflect, and act in alignment with our deepest needs without self-judgment and with grace.

Grateful for "Feeling Seen"

When one goes through life-altering events, no matter how long or short lived, it can feel lonely, isolating, and we often do it without realizing others have gone through the same or similar things that we have. And it can often feel infuriating being told "you're fine" when you know you are off.

Just as the association with medical moments and weakness is a common throughline, so is the opportunity of the gratefulness of "feeling seen." It's a moment of awakening to the commonality that exists beyond what we realize or expect.

One of the biggest gifts I have received in interviewing women is the trust they have given me with their stories, and it has been the unintentional opportunity I have been given in allowing each and every one of them to be seen. I have been told, "Reflecting on this moment and sharing this after a long time brought up a lot, and I realized how truly grateful I am to tell my story and how much I have grown from this experience of sharing." And this also opens the doors to authentic community support, which we will explore more in the next chapter.

The concept of "feeling seen" has roots in both psychological and spiritual frameworks. In his work, psychologist Carl Rogers has emphasized the importance of unconditional positive regard and the idea that truly being understood and accepted by others is foundational to human growth and healing.[1] When someone acknowledges our pain or validates our feelings, it creates a safe space for us to process and heal.

One common medical challenge that many women face is fibroids—a condition that can lead to excessive bleeding and debilitating physical and emotional effects. It often leaves women feeling isolated and ashamed, because although it's common, it's not often publicly spoken about. According to Johns Hopkins Medicine, an estimated 20–50% of women of reproductive age currently have fibroids, and up to 77% will develop them at some point during their childbearing years.[2] Yet, despite how widespread this condition is, many women struggle in silence, feeling unseen and alone as they navigate its impact on their lives.

Atoya Burleson, founder of Ladies Playbook—a digital community dedicated to providing access to unique resources and necessary support for a professional athlete's family to thrive—is one such woman who faced the all too challenging condition of having fibroids. Her challenge eventually required a hysterectomy, but not before a deeply embarrassing and isolating experience intersected with her life while she was attending a wedding and found herself unexpectedly bleeding through her clothes. The wedding reception had just started, and with nothing else to wear, she wound up back in her hotel room, isolated, ashamed, and deeply disappointed for all she would have to miss. She found herself consumed with anxiety in the days that followed, not only ashamed but wondering what was going on with her body. It was an experience that left her feeling vulnerable, paranoid, and desperate for answers.

It wasn't until she attended a woman's summit, where another woman shared a very similar experience, that her perspective began to change. She felt seen. And through that recognition, instead of continuing to put a Band-Aid on how she was feeling, and hiding her shame within, she learned to do the work, be brave, and have the conversation. That moment of connection—the realization that she was not alone and recognition that in fact many women have the same challenges—gave her a renewed perspective and shame turned into empowerment.

In many ways, feeling seen is about connection. As touched upon in Chapter 2, neuroscience shows us that humans are wired for empathy and social bonding. When we feel understood by others, our brains release oxytocin, the "love hormone," which fosters trust, reduces stress, and deepens our sense of belonging. This biochemical reaction also underscores the transformative power of shared understanding.

What's remarkable about the experience of being seen is how it often arrives in unanticipated ways. It can arrive in our most silent moments or in our moments of our most self-critical dialogues. It might be a friend who shares a story that mirrors our struggle, a stranger's empathetic smile, or even an inspiring piece of art, literature, or music that seems to articulate the very emotions we cannot name. But it is in these moments we can have transcendental change.

In these moments, feeling "seen" is not just a comfort—it can be a lifeline, because it's in these moments we recognize that we are not standing alone. We are standing in the light that others shine upon us with care and compassion of those who walk this journey with us. And even more remarkably, as we experience the gift of being seen, the ability to do that for others magnifies the power of it. It's a trait and characteristic I have witnessed in Atoya time and time again, and she continuously uplifts those around her because of it.

Today, through her leadership in Ladies Playbook—a core example of her living her purpose—she pays forward her gratefulness of being seen in her establishment of a space where spouses and significant others of NFL players can feel safe, heard, and supported throughout their year-round transitions. A space where those who have experience being an NFL spouse can share vital information and resources to other women new to the industry life at a very crucial time of their lives, reenforcing the message that no one has to navigate their journey in isolation.

Grateful for Learning the Art of Letting Go

> "I realized that sometimes, no matter how hard you try to change or control a situation, it won't budge—and there's a reason for that. Challenges and crises hold lessons that shape us in ways we don't immediately understand."
>
> **—Kristen Paladino, Founder and CEO, Paladino Casting**

In 2018, Kristen Paladino learned she had a uterine fibroid, a condition usually harmless unless untreated. Measuring just 2 cm, it initially seemed manageable. Her doctor recommended monitoring it, and if it grew, she would need to schedule surgery. She consulted a nutritionist and hired a trainer, creating a wellness plan aimed at maintaining her health and preventing the fibroid from growing. For a time, she felt optimistic. Then an ultrasound in September showed it had grown to 6 cm. By December, it had enlarged further, and her symptoms became impossible to ignore—severe bleeding disrupted her daily life, leaving her homebound during her periods.

It was evident that it was not controlled, and surgery needed to be scheduled. After consulting a few doctors, Kristen's options were traditional open C-section surgery, but due to the bleeding, she leaned toward a robotic myomectomy—a less invasive procedure with faster recovery times. That same month, she broke her shoulder, and this injury delayed her option for scheduling fibroid surgery until her shoulder was fully healed. All of this sidelined her health routines as well, leaving her physically and emotionally drained. Ultimately she settled on fibroid surgery in April 2019.

By early March 2019, she had a nagging cough that was initially dismissed as a cold but began to worsen. Kristen's basic movement was soon a struggle, and she was often winded. She coughed persistently, battled fatigue, and experienced strange symptoms, including vomiting. Even at the urging of friends and family to see a doctor, she still hesitated, telling herself that rest over the weekend would suffice.

Finally, she called the doctor. During her appointment, the gravity of the situation became clear. Her doctor insisted Kristen go to the emergency room immediately. At first she questioned this, mentioning she had a screening for work she could not miss. Her doctor's words were firm: "You must go now." At the ER, everything changed. Tests revealed an alarming diagnosis—multiple pulmonary embolisms, with blood clots in both lobes of her lungs. The seriousness of her condition hit like a tidal wave. IV blood thinners were started immediately, and she was admitted to the hospital.

She was deeply grateful for her doctors, but today she is even more grateful for the transformative lessons she learned during her enforced pause. The sudden slowdown brought worries racing through her mind: "How will my company run without me? How do I keep this private, so people don't think I'm incapable of working or leading? Will everything fall apart without my constant presence?" It was the start of a new understanding about how she affiliated her identity, and the needed shift to seeing her identity as an individual with many talents, not an identify solely defined as being the CEO of her company.

What Kristen was forced to learn is the power of letting go and delegation—a lesson that changed how she approaches her business as a founder. What started as something she had no choice in became a new empowerment. What began as an unavoidable necessity evolved into a new way of thinking and operating her life. She learned to trust her team, giving them responsibilities she previously felt compelled to handle alone. This newfound trust showed her that the company she built was strong enough to thrive even without her constant involvement in oversight. Delegation, once a reluctant effort, became a deliberate and strategic practice. And it opened space for meaningful self-care, ultimately allowing her to show up as a stronger leader. She's also learned that the self-care she had been doing at the time was more like a fight-or-flight response. She was relying on how she always operated, pushing through on adrenaline, pushing herself to extremes, an approach she had conditioned herself to do since launching her company at the age of 27, seeing her business's success as a reflection of who she was. But she has since learned that sometimes what your body really needs is stillness: simply to just be in a state of being, and you can only find space for that if you are willing to let go of other things.

Kristen's experience in many ways mirrors the journeys of Sarah Kugelman in Chapter 2, Cate Luzio in Chapter 3, Jill Katz in Chapter 4, and countless female leaders, including myself. For many of us, it is often life's most challenging moments that force us to pause and embrace the art of letting go. In doing so, we unlock the potential of our teams, discover new freedoms, and, importantly, realize that true leadership lies in empowering others.

Grateful for Accepting Uncertainty

"No amount of planning will solve all the issues."

—Mina Fader, managing director, Baker Retailing Center

Life often unfolds in ways we cannot predict, despite our best efforts to plan every detail. For Mina Fader, managing director at the Baker Retailing Center at the Wharton School of the University of Pennsylvania, this lesson became deeply personal through two pivotal experiences. One involved the birth of her second child, an event that deviated sharply from her expectations. The other was the responsibility of caring for her aging parents. Each of these moments reshaped her perspective on control, uncertainty, and the idea of perfection.

When Mina was preparing to give birth to her second child, she assumed she would have the option of pain management, just as she had meticulously planned. But in a sudden twist, a medical emergency dictated otherwise. She was informed that she could not receive an epidural, a revelation that forced her to confront the situation with no alternative but to endure it fully. At that moment, fear and frustration could have taken over. Instead, she realized that resistance would only heighten her suffering. By accepting the circumstances as they were, she was able to find an unexpected strength within herself. The experience taught her that sometimes, despite our best-laid plans, life forces us to surrender to what is. And in that surrender, we often find resilience we never knew we had.

Later in life, Mina found herself in another transformative role: that of a caregiver for her ailing parents. Watching loved ones grow frail is an emotional challenge that many people face. Caregiving is unpredictable; no manual or plan can fully prepare a person for the emotional toll it takes. In supporting her parents, Mina realized that perfection was an illusion—there was no "right" way to navigate this journey. Some days were filled with patience and grace; others were heavy with exhaustion and doubt. But through it all, she discovered a new kind of strength: the ability to embrace imperfection, to do her best without the constant need to control outcomes, and to offer herself the same compassion she extended to her parents. And in that, she began to embrace the mindset of "what we had was really great," an acknowledgment that allowed her to let go of the relentless urge to always push and push in all she does.

For much of her life, Mina was accustomed to structure and planning. Her professional success was built on strategic thinking, problem-solving, and anticipating challenges before they arose. Yet through these deeply personal experiences, she learned that not every challenge is meant to be solved. Some situations require adaptation rather than control, acceptance rather than resistance. This realization freed her in ways she had never anticipated. She unlocked a new truth for herself: Perfection is not the goal. Life is unpredictable, and while planning is useful, it is not a safeguard against the unexpected. There will always be moments when we must step into uncertainty with faith rather than fear. And there will be some times when letting go is the wisest choice we can make.

Grateful for Self-Exploration

Self-exploration is an ongoing journey. It happens at any life stage and when we can embrace it, we can uncover wonderful things about ourselves.

In her retirement, Alexis Thomas—former executive, senior advisor, and a woman whose impressive career includes roles like principal and fixed income syndicate manager, commissioner of the New York State Insurance Fund, and senior advisor of Douglass Park Asset Management—finally found time to embark on a journey that had long been waiting for her: a six-week mostly solo adventure to Paris.

For much of her life, Alexis's calendar was packed with commitments to others—serving, supporting, advising, and showing up. But this trip was a time for her to show up for herself. It was a journey and a space to explore the new territories of her inner self, alongside the backdrop of the vibrant and romantic city of Paris. It also marked the birth of what she fondly refers to as "the new adventure girl."

In Paris, Alexis allowed herself to step into a different rhythm, one dictated not by responsibilities but by curiosity and joy. Spending weeks being explorative, she did everything from staying in non-touristy corners of the city and taking in local life to indulging in an extravagant stay at a boutique hotel she would never have otherwise treated herself to. A tennis enthusiast, she attended the French Open, taking in the international experience. And holistically she embraced the art of wandering—without an hour-to-hour, day-by-day agenda. It was a trip purposefully created in its unstructured nature. Alexis spent hours in cafés where English was rarely spoken, sipping coffee and taking in the flow of Parisian life. She let herself be a student again, picking up pieces of the French language and absorbing the culture and a different way of life.

For Alexis, the trip wasn't just about seeing Paris—it was about rediscovering herself. She realized she had more of an explorer's spirit than she ever imagined. She learned she could cherish time alone and find beauty in every small detail of the journey. An avid shopper who values her fashion, she packed so lightly she would need to do laundry and visit dry cleaners during her stay, and learned she doesn't need "all her things" around her to be happy. She learned in her trip, in her journey of self-exploration, that there is the arrival of choice and fulfillment. And while this was her first trip like this, it was really just the start of a new perspective—a new way of thinking of travel and discovery. And Italy is already next on the list.

Taking time to step away from the familiar and immerse ourselves in new experiences can allow us to reconnect with who we are at our core. It creates space for growth, renewal, and the discovery of untapped potential. Every time we embark on a new experience, a new trip, we open the opportunity for this discovery. And research shows that self-exploration—whether through travel, reflection, or stepping out of our comfort zones—has profound psychological benefits[3] and individuals who engage in self-reflection and exploration report higher levels of self-awareness and fulfillment. Moreover, self-exploration gives us the opportunity to redefine what truly matters, a tool we can use in our roadmap to purpose, as explored in Chapter 4. It allows us to ask ourselves questions like "*What brings me joy? What makes me feel whole?*" In Alexis's journey, she could shine a light on the value of living intentionally and making choices that align with personal desires rather than external pulls and expectations.

Self-exploration is accessible to all of us, as is finding things we are grateful for. While these examples are just a starter list of gratitude stories and lessons, it can prompt your own thought process and journey. Sometimes those things we are most grateful for can be conjured from within, and other times it is through the generosity and wisdom of others.

For our first exercise in this chapter let's create your year of gratitude exploration.

Gratitude Jug

Each time you feel thankful for something, jot that feeling on a piece of paper and place it in a jar; or create a list in the notes app of your phone and store your gratitude thoughts as you have them.

At the end of each month, read them back to yourself.

At the end of the year, read them all again.

Reflect: What have you learned about what you stored in your jar? What concepts of gratitude does it help you illuminate?

As we find gratitude, we also find grace. And the power of giving yourself grace has both psychological and emotional benefits. Grace encourages an emotional strength and resilience because it allows us to acknowledge human fallibility, our capacity to be imperfect with acceptance.[4] Additionally, when we allow ourselves to release ourselves from the burden of perfectionist tendencies, we create space for personal growth and mental well-being. Studies highlight that individuals who practice self-grace also experience lower levels of stress and anxiety.[5] They are more forgiving to themselves and permit errors without or with less self-judgment and embrace challenge without fear of judgment or failure.

> "If I'm willing to take the risk, I have to be ready to own and reconcile the consequences, know everything isn't rosy, and ask myself, what did I learn and I will I apply it the next time to be smarter and better."
>
> **—Rebecca Minkoff, author of the bestselling book *Fearless* and host of *Superwomen* podcast**

In the rest of this chapter, we will explore the power of grace and spirituality, the concept of when self-love is the needed medicine. In this exploration we can uncover more deeply how the practice of self-grace can empower us to reclaim our personal narratives and move beyond self-imposed limitations. This reclaim contributes to a sense of agency and authenticity in our personal growth.

Finding Grace Through the Power of Spirituality

> "We are spiritual beings first."
>
> **—Tai Beauchamp, founder, Morning Mindset with Tai**

Grace is often discussed in theological and philosophical contexts as a divine or universal quality. Spirituality often sits adjacent to that capability as a vehicle toward cultivating inner peace and interconnectedness. Offering practical tools for personal development, it can allow us to define a path based on values and foster a sense of belonging.

As a destination that "always called her," Tai Beauchamp, founder of Morning Mindset with Tai, sought solace in a refuge in Bali when she realized she needed an arrested pause in her life. She was at a crossroads of burnout and anxiety, launching and growing two businesses, no longer feeling centered. Bali would be her path to deeply rediscovering her center.

Bali is often described as the "Island of the Gods." Balinese culture is steeped in an ever-present spirituality that finds expression in the daily rhythm of life, from the intricate offerings placed on doorsteps to the elaborate temple ceremonies that seem to happen on every corner. Watching these rituals, or respectfully participating, visitors are gently reminded of the power of collective devotion and spiritual harmony. If one is seeking spiritual growth, Bali's unique blend of religion, focus on humanity, love of all living beings, and longstanding traditions are known to be deeply supportive in that journey. Tai was cognizant that in a season of overwhelm she required a journey into the practice of gratitude, humility, and mindfulness—cornerstones of many spiritual paths.

Never having taken a vacation for more than 10 days, Tai was thrust into a longer break than she had planned on when divine intervention stepped in, and her assistant accidentally booked a trip for dates spanning almost nine weeks rather than just four. She embraced this as "well, maybe that's what is meant to be." She waited until the last minute (three weeks before traveling) to book and was guided by a friend who lives in Bali to book a new resort that had a very small social footprint at the time. Trusting her friend, moving into a state of flow, she accepted her friend's recommendation and introduction. Upon arrival, the trip became a more profound gift and reset than she expected, energetically thrusting her into a new zone. Taking refuge in a highly spiritual destination, one she characterizes as living a life under the *Entourage* (the HBO show) filter—"bright, glossy, with a subtle softness that gives an 'endless summer' aspirational feel," Tai eased into a life of flow, ease, and peace, one almost antithetical to the one she lived as a too-busy "boss woman" in New York and Los Angeles.

Referencing the saying "Birds of a feather flock together," Tai found her connection to her own spirituality heightened daily, supported by gatherings among like-minded people and the opportunity it gives to elevate your beliefs and practice. She embarked on a three-day prayer pilgrimage, visiting 11 of the 11,000+ temples the small island is home to. No matter how grand or small, each was an anchoring point for offerings, prayer, and community gatherings. Through these simple but intentional visits, she gained a new understanding and appreciation of what life is like when spirituality is not separate from everyday living. With burnout, she realized, sometimes one has to sticker-shock their way into healing and recalibration. And with that she gained a clearer and more pronounced lens on life, and it ushered her into a new way of being. This didn't replace her spirituality anchored in Christian beliefs or teachings that framed her childhood, but these experiences enhanced and even illuminated the power of faith, peace, love, and acceptance—values that are universally taught in each religion.

Part of Bali's spiritual allure comes from its tradition of holistic well-being. And with that comes the practice of rituals: lighting incense, putting out flowers, offering ceremonies and blessings, as well as more traditional healing methods from local healers, known as "balian," experiencing the power of herbal remedies and energy work. Even the practice of making and placing small offerings, called *canang sari*, became a profound example of gestures of gratitude to remind Tai to slow down and appreciate each moment. It not only gave her a new centering as an individual, it also informed how she approaches her Morning Mindset with Tai offering to others.

Allowing spirituality in can encourage self-reflection and support the development of virtues such as compassion, empathy, and mindfulness, all of which lead to personal empowerment. In more recent years, spirituality, especially nonreligious forms, has garnered widespread attention, with individuals across diverse cultures and lifestyles turning to spiritual practices as a means to enhance well-being, resilience, and personal fulfillment. This adaptability has made a connection to spirituality accessible and relatable.

The effectiveness of these practices lies in their holistic approach to addressing modern challenges by integrating mental, emotional, and existential dimensions of life, like what Tai experienced in Bali. Often facilitated through practices such as meditation, mindfulness, breathwork, yoga, and affirmations (for which we have a worksheet at the end of this book), it allows for an accessible means of connectedness to oneself. It's a methodology that can improve mental health, bringing a deeper level of self-awareness and emotional regulation. Tai calls this directing focus to being, rather than doing.

Studies have also shown significant reductions in anxiety, depression, and stress among individuals who incorporate mindfulness and meditation into their daily lives.[6] By encouraging introspection and acceptance, we can gain new tools to navigate personal and professional challenges with a greater degree of mental calmness and even temper. In a technological, always-on world, where we experience stress, increasingly higher demands, and burnout, it also encourages a disconnection, stillness, and presence, to break the unhealthy fixation we have of constantly seeking empty fixes that often lead to a lack of fulfillment. It can give solace and promote inner peace and a reprieve by helping us focus on the present and detach from external pressures.

For Tai, her spiritual journey has not only allowed more introspection but has also allowed her to live her life with more patience than in the past and has given her the ability to become less attached to the outcomes living with appreciation of the losses and gains and how they both enrich her life holistically. A trip that she scheduled to give her clarity and pause gave her a different level of resolve she didn't know before. The pause allowed her to center, discover, and trust how she wanted to own grace as a way of life. Since her first trip, she has returned to host others—28 women to be exact—on a 10-day spirituality journey and plans to make that part of her ongoing practice to share her learnings with others. She will host another retreat in Bali in December 2025. In addition to her own personal reset, she was grateful to see how Bali also affirmed what she had been doing to develop and grow Morning Mindset with Tai. She was reminded that the pillars she established for MMWT back in 2020 were not only powerful but spiritually aligned with values that ultimately support peace and enlightenment. Bali proved that!

> Today, here are the foundational elements of Morning Mindset with Tai:
>
> - Affirm yourself, affirm others, nature, God, or source; declare and speak your words.
> - Move your body (healthy bodies are essential) and shift your energy and let it flow.
> - Reset: Be still and find peace.

For Tai, rituals breed the way she lives life, having a place and role, not of control but of love and humanity. And admittedly, when she doesn't practice the said rituals with consistency, she feels off kilter.

The benefit of leaning into one's spirituality is personal and powerful. Through spiritual practice (not necessarily religious practices), Tai is certain that enhanced mental well-being is guaranteed. Studies show that people with a strong sense of spirituality tend to be more resilient to depression, anxiety, and stress. This is because it fosters adaptive mechanisms in the brain, helping us find meaning and growth through challenges[7] and thus can help us along our journey. This is very much the case in terms of how we embrace the opportunity of Growth Wisdom, as explored in Chapter 4. According to Lisa Miller, PhD, author of *An Awakened Brain*, the brain has the capacity to "awaken" through regular spiritual practices such as prayer, meditation, or mindfulness. This is because these practices can promote neuroplasticity, helping the brain adapt and develop pathways that support joy and resilience, because it's the personal experience of transcendence and connectedness that awakens the brain.

Well-being is not just physical, emotional, financial, or social. It encompasses eight key forms, and spiritual wellness is not only one of those forms, but for Tai it is the cornerstone. What your cornerstone and foundational catalyst is for total well-being may be different than Tai. But she's keen to remind us that, at our core, we are spiritual beings first.

When Self-Love Is the Needed Medicine, Grace Starts Within

"It's a challenge for me to give myself grace."

—Numerous women interviewed

When one is open to spirituality, they also embark on an intentional journey of reflection and acceptance, one that invites a mental and emotional review of their experiences and how they shape their sense of self. This process, though deeply personal, carries universal lessons about the importance of giving oneself grace.

I have witnessed this transformative practice firsthand through my mother, Clarissa Ramos-Cafarelli. A woman of remarkable resilience, she has approached life with a spiritual lens that fosters gratitude, alignment with purpose, and inner peace. These are not abstract concepts, but tools that enhance our mental well-being and deepen our connection to self-presence. As we grow into a more grounded understanding of who we are, we find greater trust in our purpose and an openness to releasing what no longer serves us. This is a process of shedding and making space for energy that fuels us—a concept we will explore further in Chapter 9.

Throughout her career in both the nonprofit and private sectors, my mother has meaningfully aimed to deepen her inner strength in order to enable her own personal growth and to lift others with empathy and accountability. She is a well-accomplished executive with a focus on coaching, talent management, and inclusion. Her strategies, tailored to the unique needs of each person, emphasize a path to holistic growth and impactful leadership. Yet even with decades of experience coaching others, giving herself grace has been an evolving practice—one that she works to nurture with intentionality, courage, and her own relationship to spirituality.

> Through spirituality, my mother has learned to embrace critical questions:
>
> - What did I make happen?
> - How much of what I hold onto is due to what happened to me, and how can I let go of that?
> - How have I been impacted by those who lack empathy and care, and how can I heal from those wounds?

These questions are not always easy to ask on a personal level yet can be essential for growth. They invite reflection not only on accomplishments but also on the burdens we carry—the mistakes, the hurts, and the expectations that weigh us down. Giving oneself grace means acknowledging these truths without judgment. It is about understanding that growth is not linear, and progress is not perfection.

For my mother, this practice of self-compassion allows her to apply what she did so well in her professional career and channel that thought process to "sort her life into metaphorical boxes." Some boxes remain closed, their contents processed and acknowledged but not held onto. Others are opened carefully, when the time and space feel right. This approach has become an act of grace itself, choosing when and how to confront the past while honoring the present.

Giving yourself grace, as my mother exemplifies, is not about excusing yourself from responsibility or glossing over hardships. It is about holding yourself with the same kindness you would extend to a close friend or beloved family member. And it also demonstrates the importance of gratitude, both for the progress she has made and for the moments that have shaped her into the person she is today: a mother, grandmother, a wife, and an accomplished professional. Gratitude, paired with grace, becomes a powerful practice of acceptance. It allows us to view our lives not through the lens of what we lack but through the abundance of what we have learned and gained.

Breaking Down to Build Back Up

> "When you are in it—living the life of a high performer—you don't even realize you're under stress because you've conditioned yourself to believe that the pressure is normal."
>
> **—Kendra Bracken-Ferguson, founder of Brain Trust and BrainTrust Fund**

During an intimate conversation with me in her New York City hotel room, Kendra Bracken-Ferguson reflected on a pivotal period in her life, a moment when she realized how much self-love, faith, and grace were the medicines she desperately needed.

I first met Kendra over a decade ago through a fellow entrepreneur at WeWork, when she was co-founder of Digital Brand Architects (DBA), a groundbreaking management agency that redefined the influencer marketing space and was later sold to United Talent Artist Agency (UTA). Since then Kendra has accomplished so much, launching BrainTrust, which encompasses BrainTrust Agency, a digital marketing and brand development consultancy; BrainTrust Founders Studio, the largest membership-based platform for inclusive founders in beauty and wellness; and BrainTrust Fund I, a traditional $15MM venture fund. She is a transformative brand builder, visionary leader, and a proven secret ingredient in guiding and monetizing more than 200 influencer-driven brands that have collectively generated more than $100M in revenue. In 2024, she became a best-selling author with the debut of her first book, *The Beauty of Success: Start, Grow and Accelerate Your Brand,* which was named the number one new release in business entrepreneurship on Amazon, and she stepped into a new chapter as the CEO of a publicly traded bio-aesthetics company.

From the outside, her life seemed like a highlight reel: thriving career, industry influence, and an inspiring entrepreneurial journey. But behind the scenes, her body and spirit were sending messages she could no longer ignore.

Kendra began noticing changes that shook her confidence. Severe acne slowly began erupting across her face, a first for someone who had never experienced skin issues. And as someone leading a beauty product–focused organization, her self-esteem took a hit. "I couldn't recognize myself," she admitted, "and it affected the way I saw my value."

As she dug deeper, meeting with doctors, she realized the breakouts weren't random. They mirrored the stress she had unknowingly carried into her new role. She began to see a pattern: Every time she stepped into an environment misaligned with her personal pillars and talents, her body literally resisted. The high-performance lifestyle she'd built around "handling it all" no longer sustained her. Her once-reliable outlets—exercise, meditation, mindful eating—had been sidelined in favor of work that was depleting her rather than replenishing her. The stress was manifesting physically: acne on her forehead pointed to stress; hormonal breakouts on her chin compounded the problem. When Kendra visited her doctor, she was asked a simple but powerful question: "What's going on in your life?" The floodgates opened. Uncontrollable tears, a racing heart, and a deep, overwhelming sadness poured out of her. She was experiencing not just emotional stress but physical burnout. Her body was desperately crying for relief.

This breakdown became a breakthrough. Kendra tapped into her spirituality and asked for permission to tap out and reset, not just physically, but mentally. For the first time, she shifted her prayers from asking for solutions to asking for alignment. She prayed for circumstances that would serve her, spaces where she could find grace and abundance. "It was a moment of surrender" for her and she realized the opportunity to stop pushing and start listening.

By listening and giving herself grace, she recognized she became caught in the pursuit of superficial things and had abandoned what truly drives her, which was guided by her long-standing pillars—community, mentorship, and education—and ultimately to be of service to her community, to be an entrepreneur for entrepreneurs, to be a builder and visionary. Through reflection, she realized that her stress stemmed not just from the pressures of work but from losing sight of her purpose. Today Kendra is embracing her full self, her talents, and her passions, starting with how she views herself in the mirror.

Her skin journey became symbolic of her inner transformation, in both directions. And instead of perpetuating negativity by criticizing her skin pigmentations, she reaffirms with gratitude and kindness. She looks in the mirror and says, "Thank you. You are beautiful. We are healing. We are prosperous. We are fine." These affirmations, though simple, have enabled her to move forward with grace. And they are an anchor, reminding her that faith, self-compassion, and self-love are the keys to a life well lived.

An Artistic Journey to Finding Self-Love and Grace

> "When a woman reclaims her voice and her sense of self-worth, it doesn't just change her life—it impacts everyone around her."
>
> **—Chiara Mecozzi, artist, photographer, collagist, and mixed-media painter**

There are many paths one can take to find self-love, grace, and healing. Many of us will cry at some point of the journey, some will travel to new places like Paris and Bali, others will seek therapy or outlets such as meditation. In this story of artist, photographer, collagist, and mixed-media painter Chiara Mecozzi, I found a uniquely bold journey from a woman overcoming her own personal trauma to one who now finds herself rooted in empowerment, liberation, and self-worth, not just for herself but for other women as well.

For much of her life, Chiara lived disconnected from her body and her sense of self. Growing up immersed in Latina culture, she was surrounded by the deeply ingrained values of machismo and societal expectations that often placed a woman's worth on how she appeared or served others. From an early age, she was taught—implicitly and explicitly—to prioritize what others thought of her above her own feelings or needs. This mindset shaped every aspect of Chiara's life, from how she dressed to how she behaved. And as a result, she often was trapped by the need for external validation, trying to mold herself into what she thought others wanted.

Chiara's relentless pursuit of approval, paired with the cultural pressure to please and conform, chipped away at her sense of individuality.

She felt she had to be restrained, accommodating, and self-sacrificing in order to fit into the roles expected of her. Over time, she lost touch with her own desires and needs, believing her worth was entirely tied to how others perceived her. She lived in a constant state of unease, masking her true self to avoid rejection or judgment, and this created a woman unable to stand confidently in her own skin, disabling her from stepping into her power.

At a pivotal point in her life, as her marriage was ending, Chiara found herself with a wake-up call to reconnect with her inner self. One day, as she stepped out of the shower, she caught herself criticizing her reflection in the mirror. In that moment, as negative thoughts about her body surfaced, she made a powerful decision: she would no longer allow those thoughts to define her. Instead, she chose to change the way she thought of and saw herself, using photography as a tool of transformation and neuroplasticity—a way to rewire her mind and redefine her relationship with her body by facing her vulnerable, naked self directly through the lens of her camera.

This profound act of photographing herself, raw and unfiltered, was terrifying at first, she shared. But as she later looked at the photographs she was brave enough to take, something unexpected happened: She began to see herself differently. The shame and judgment she carried for so long began to give way to compassion and curiosity. Inspired by the newfound feeling of self-love she experienced with these photographs, she began creating collages intertwined with macro photographs of flowers and plants—images she had taken that felt deeply personal and alive. These flowers, with their intricate details and forms, she found often resembled parts of the human body, blurring the lines between the organic world and her own physicality. This process felt intimate and healing, as if she were piecing together fragments of herself and uncovering beauty in places she had once ignored or rejected.

Collaging then led to painting. Using her photographed images as references and guides, she translated them onto canvas, allowing her to confront her body in a new and transformative way. The act of painting became a dialogue with herself—a way to process pain, celebrate resilience, and reclaim her power. When she saw the first painting of her naked body, she felt something she had never felt before: a new sense of love and liberation. For the first time, she saw her body not as a source of shame but as a vessel of strength and beauty.

Today, she shares this gift of empowerment, self-love, and grace with women all over. In 2020, she was invited to exhibit her work at the Argentine Consulate of New York. Thirteen paintings of her naked body were displayed, telling her story of disentangling shame and pain and transforming it into healing, liberation, and empowerment. And while sharing this deeply personal work and her story was both terrifying and exhilarating, it opened the door for connection and understanding of her newfound purpose behind her work. As women approached her after the exhibition, sharing their own struggles with body image and self-worth, this marked a new beginning of her work with women, a mission that she continues today, in celebration of resilience and transformation.

The Opportunity of Prescence

> "You can't beat yourself up and dwell in the negative, but rather trust you are where you are meant to be and it's not a linear line."
>
> **—Antonia Saint Dunbar, Co-Founder of THINX, Antonia Saint New York**

In 2005, Antonia Saint Dunbar, well known as co-founder of the innovative company THINX, gained a whole new appreciation of the power of presence and spirituality when she survived a potentially catastrophic car accident on her way to a spiritual retreat she was attending with friends. On a foggy, rainy morning, the car she was in lost control and veered through six lanes of traffic, nearly colliding with a swerving semi-truck coming their way. They went flying through the air and were left suspended from bushes on the edge of a ravine, but miraculously only their back bumper was nicked with the paint of one oncoming car, and there were no fatalities or even serious injuries. In that moment, she gained a new acceptance that there is "always the hand of a higher universal power" co-creating life with you, and that life was indeed precious. It gave her a new appreciation for every moment that was available to cultivate presence, and it spurred within her a resolve to finally uncover her purpose in this life. It was the ignition of her journey as a spiritual being who really knew that the gifts of time and possibility could shift in an instant. And in the aftermath of this terrifying experience, everything came sharply into focus, where every aspect of life sought meaning and presence.

As touched upon in Chapter 1, presence is more than physical proximity; it is the state of being fully engaged in the here and now. Eckhart Tolle,[8] a renowned spiritual teacher known for his seminal works *The Power of Now* and *A New Earth*, emphasizes living in the present moment as the path to spiritual awakening. He believes the root of much human suffering lies in identification with the ego and compulsive thinking (which is often triggered when engaging with social platforms). He describes presence as "a state of inner stillness and alertness."

In our fast-paced, hyper-connected world, the concept of presence often feels elusive and difficult to achieve. We are well conditioned to dwell in the past or obsess over the future, but the present moment holds a unique opportunity and is a portal to grace and spiritual awakening. With presence, we unlock the ability to experience life with clarity and gratitude. In moments, like the one Antonia faced with friends, that state of clarity also becomes a portal into introspection and discovery.

In practical terms, presence means actively listening to someone else without formulating your opinions or bias while they speak. It means noticing the textures and flavors of a meal instead of mindlessly shoving food in your face. It means savoring the sound of rustling leaves or the song of birds chirping on a quiet morning. Often it can take an experience as jolting as an accident or medical trauma to realign our relationship with presence, but we can also begin the practice of it just by embracing the details of seemingly mundane moments.

As we embrace the power of presence, we also more deeply see the importance of grace and mindfulness, especially in its ability to overcome challenges. It enables us to see that progress and evolution come in small, incremental steps; it won't happen in one day. And if we listen closely enough, we see that life is full of wake-up calls, lessons, and reminders. For Antonia, it was in her convergence with the thought of seeing her life flash before her eyes. For me, it was my experience where I had to absorb my doctor's every word as he shared my emergency options and I felt the whole world around me stop. Presence can serve as a catalyst for awakening. It's a grounding of ourselves in the now when we become more deeply attuned to the truths of existence in a meaningful way.

When we find presence, we also open a new pathway to accessing wisdom—wisdom that goes beyond intellectual understanding—and it allows us to quiet the noise of fear and doubt and opens us to hear and trust intuition a little more.

Presence as a Path to Leadership Growth

As we tie it all together—gratitude, grace, spirituality, and presence—we begin to add to the building blocks that support our path toward growth not only personally but also as leaders. Presence is not just about being physically available; it is about showing up mentally, emotionally, and spiritually. By cultivating presence, leaders can grow into their roles with authenticity, empathy, and resilience, inspiring others to do the same. And it's a practice that can transcend us both personally and professionally.

One leader who constantly inspires me with her gift of presence is Mindy Grossman, partner and vice-chair of Consello Group. A woman of enormous accomplishments, she contributed various thoughts and insights in this book. I often witness Mindy's gift of attentive listening and presence, and I am in awe of it. I also believe her ability of presence has supported her continuous professional success, a road she has taken with humility and grace.

Mindy's career spans transformative roles in global retail, wellness, and consumer-driven industries. As the former president and CEO of WW International (formerly Weight Watchers), she aimed to shift the company's focus from solely dieting to overall well-being. This strategic move included rebranding the company as WW in 2018, emphasizing a holistic approach to health and wellness. She was praised by Oprah Winfrey as a "bold marketing visionary" who transformed the brand to represent the many dimensions of weight loss and wellness because of her ability to hear what people needed and were craving, and her talent for taking those insights to adapt the organization. Prior to WW, Mindy was a key figure in organizations like HSNi, where she served as CEO and transformed the company into a $4 billion direct-to-consumer content and commerce leader, and Nike, where she served as global vice president of apparel and revitalized Nike's apparel division by reengineering the organization and introducing sub-brands like Nike Performance, Nike Active, and Nike Fusion and driving apparel revenue from $2.7 billion to $4.1 billion in five years. Through her unwavering gift of presence, Mindy has consistently driven innovation, growth, and cultural transformation with a leadership style that fosters inclusion and impact through her power of listening.

Presence is the art of being completely in tune with the here and now. In leadership, this means actively listening to your team, your peers, and your customers, making thoughtful decisions without distraction, and responding to challenges with clarity. Leaders who practice presence have the ability to create impact beyond themselves. Their clarity and calm fosters trust, it instills a sense of "feeling seen" to those around them, and it consequently creates a sense of empowerment and inspires confidence. Presence also sharpens self-awareness and fosters empathy, as it illustrates the ability to understand and share the feelings of others. By paying attention to the words and thoughts of others, leaders can hear the emotions and behaviors and gain a better understanding of how they influence others. In his book *Primal Leadership*, Daniel Goleman argues that leaders who understand themselves can align their actions with their values, and this creates authenticity and trust. Furthermore, in a world where chaos can creep in, presence allows for clear thinking that cuts through the noise that can often cloud us. When leaders focus on the present moment, they can assess situations more objectively and make decisions based on facts rather than fear or biased assumptions. This allows for decision-making that isn't burdened with ruminating on past mistakes or feeling frozen by the worry of future challenges. Present-focused leaders face challenges with grace and adapt more effectively.

Rituals and Practical Ways to Cultivate Presence

Mindfulness practices: Find a practice—whether it's meditation, mindful breathing, or sound baths—that allows you to focus on the now without judgment.

Active listening: Practice opportunities to make eye contact, no multitasking, no judging as someone is speaking to you, just listening. Test yourself by summarizing what was said to gauge what you have captured.

Self-reflection: Try journaling or a form of capture to reflect and process your experiences and associated emotions. Ask yourself questions such as: What was a success today? What was my Achilles' heel?

Scheduled digital detoxes: Schedule time daily to disconnect, allowing you to fully engage in the active moments you are in, separating yourself from inactive engagements.

Chapter 5 Contributors:

Lolita Lopez, Atoya Burleson, Kristen Paladino, Mina Fader, Alexis Thomas, Tai Beauchamp, Clarissa Ramos-Cafarelli, Cate Luzio, Kendra Bracken-Ferguson, Chiara Mecozzi, Antonia Saint Dunbar, Mindy Grossman

6

The Power of Community and Sisterhood

Building Meaningful Connections and the Right Support Networks

In many ways, my medical journey and the process of writing this book have been testaments to the power of community and sisterhood. Being 3,000 miles from home when I was jolted out of sleep and rushed to the ER, I was surrounded not by my biological family but by the unwavering care of my local work family and my chosen family that mobilized immediately to support me. They took shifts around the clock to ensure I had everything I needed to fill in the gaps until my husband and daughter could join me. My sister-in-law in California and my best friend from college (who was living in New York) booked flights without hesitation—choosing action over permission—to stand by my side when my husband had to travel back and forth with my daughter and while my parents couldn't travel due to being homebound with COVID.

These moments of support were not just acts of kindness; they were demonstrations of the immense power of connection and humanity that binds people together. Similarly, the women who cheered for and contributed to this book have shown me the beauty of collective strength. By sharing their vulnerabilities, experiences, and wisdom, they've elevated this project into a mini movement exemplary of the transformative potential of community. Their stories underscore a truth I've come to embrace: our connections with others can be our greatest sources of strength, insight, and resilience.

In moments of fear, of resilience, of evolution and metamorphosis, we see that community and sisterhood take many forms. They are found in family, professional networks, friendships, churches, hobbies, and more. Some communities are enduring and deeply interwoven into our lives, while others are transient yet impactful. There are groups formed through shared struggles, providing solace through empathy and mutual understanding. In some, we may share our stories with complete openness; in others, we may carefully choose what we disclose. Each relationship holds value in its own unique way, contributing to our growth and well-being.

Through my life journey, I've come to appreciate how these varied connections enrich our lives. In professional spaces like DealMakeHers (the group I introduce in the preface, and where the recognition of my health journey began), I've experienced relationships that transition seamlessly from tactical business discussions to deeply personal conversations about mental wellness and self-care. Whether at a salon-style gathering at the New York apartment of Mindy Grossman (whom you met in Chapter 5), or at a book launch event at Stacy Bern's office (whom I introduced in the preface), or standing at the NASDAQ ringing the opening bell together, or together for a 48-hour trip like those masterminded by Nancy Berger (whom you met in Chapter 1), where we experience everything from deep breathwork to cold plunges and multi-hour hikes, together we undergo deep individual exploration as an intimate group for both personal development as well as collective empowerment.

Outside of professional networks, personal friendships provide a different kind of nourishment. There are the people who mobilize at a moment's notice when "duty" calls—physically or digitally—offering exactly what you need, whether that's calm guidance, spiritual insight, or the simple joy of letting loose. Some will be your 911 call (Alice Kim, founder of PerfectDD, calls this your 911 Circle), filled with friends who can handle intense situations with calm and tactical means; some will be your deeply spiritual warriors who can go deep with you when you need it; some will be the friends you just need to let dance on tables and get a little crazy, channeling your forever youthful energy; some will see you for all that you are, every gift and every flaw and embrace all elements; some may only understand fractions of you but that's okay because those are your fractions of deepest connection with them and where you need them most. Some will have the gift of seeing life through rose-colored glasses, no matter what you tell them; others will be your tough love friends who provide the healthy tension you need in certain moments to challenge you and bring out the best in you, fostering your growth. Together, all the pockets of people in our life form a mosaic of support that meets us where we are and challenge us to be our best.

From personal to professional, women-oriented communities like Luminary, founded by Cate Luzio (whom we met in Chapter 3), and DealMakeHers, founded by Stacy Berns, Stacey Widlitz, and Mary Ann Domuracki, further remind us that shared vulnerability can transform relationships into reservoirs of strength and inspiration. In these spaces, individual well-being is nurtured alongside collective growth, creating opportunities for like-minded connection and mutual uplift. They let us ask questions without judgment, open doors for one another, and gain confidence in asking for the things we want.

> "We need to prioritize building relationships with other women. It's not a nice to have, it's not just a 'girl power kind of thing.'"
>
> **—Kelly Hoey, author, *Build Your Dream Network***

This is how social science plays out: If you have big aspirations, whether you are an entrepreneur, a lawyer, rising in the ranks of management, an educator, or seeking to succeed in a creative industry, studies show that the women who achieve more of what they are seeking, in comparison to their equally talented and ambitious peers, are those who prioritize networking with other women.[1] In pursuit of our individual interests, if we operate differently and we prioritize networking with other women, we will collectively lift up more women.

In this chapter, we will explore the opportunities we find in embracing communities, networks, and sisterhoods that serve the different roles we have in our evolving lives. When we learn to embrace the diversity of our relationships, we open ourselves to a broader spectrum of possibilities. These connections encourage us to pursue diverse interests, foster ambitions, and explore new perspectives without judgment. By weaving in and out of supportive networks, we create a life enriched by shared purpose, personal growth, and limitless potential. And we begin to embrace pockets of people who fuel personal goals and growth without stigmas.

The Metamorphic Power of Support

Trish Barillas, author of *The Face of Anxiety* and an active life coach, didn't always have a strong connection to community or the ability to forge deep relationships the way she does today. Having unknowingly struggled with anxiety disorder since the age of five, it wasn't until she was 37 that she truly learned that living in a constant flight-or-fight mode wasn't how everyone else in the world lived their daily lives.

By the age of 19, her anxiety left her weighing barely 80 pounds, and she dropped out of her sophomore year of college midsemester due to its debilitating grip. Her world grew smaller, eventually leading to agoraphobia. This marked the first time she truly acknowledged the disorder for what it was, yet shame silenced her voice and prevented her from seeking the community and help she so desperately needed. Growing up in a household that wasn't educated enough in mental health or the use of medication for mental health issues further compounded her struggle.

Despite these barriers, Trish's healing journey took a surprising turn when she found solace in an unexpected place: the nightlife scene. Amid the pulsating rhythms of music and the collective energy of strangers, she discovered moments of peace. These experiences provided her with a paradoxical sanctuary—she could feel alone yet connected at the same time. It was a precursor to understanding that connection comes in many forms, sometimes from places we least expect.

Trish struggled with the hold her anxiety had on her until she found herself home one afternoon watching the movie *Silver Linings Playbook*. "One never knows what will trigger and resonate." A scene featuring Bradley Cooper resonated deeply, where his character grappled with chaos and struggled without the help of his medication. This moment of relatability flipped a switch within her, leading her to finally confront the shame she carried about seeking medical intervention. Trish decided to explore the use of medication, not as a cure-all but as a tool to stabilize her mental health. "Medication isn't a magic solution," she often says. "It's one piece of the puzzle. You still have to do the work."

Through her own transformation, she wrote *A Face of Anxiety: Embrace Anxiety and Take Back Your Life*. In this candid memoir, infused with humor, she demystifies anxiety and offers readers actionable advice. Through her experiences with generalized anxiety disorder (GAD) and panic attacks, she tackles topics ranging from major life decisions to career transitions and romantic relationships. Her goal: to destigmatize mental health and provide a roadmap for others facing similar struggles.

By sharing her personal narrative, Trish aimed to break the stigma surrounding mental health issues, and consequently transformed from a woman trapped by fear and anxiety into a woman at the nucleus of a new community of people she was helping empower, providing readers of her work with a sense of solidarity with attainable advice to reclaim their lives from the grips of anxiety.

> "When you face your fears out loud, those fears lose their power. You realize the fear you hold is worse than the reality you fear."
>
> **—Trish Barillas**

Through her work, Trish not only found community, but she created one. And she learned one of the most substantial lessons in her journey was the immeasurable power of community. What began as an isolated struggle evolved into a mission to connect, empower, and uplift others. By sharing her story and encouraging others to speak openly about their fears, she discovered that vulnerability can be the cornerstone of meaningful relationships. Her vulnerability gave others permission to share their own struggles, and together they built networks of mutual understanding and growth.

Trish's journey teaches us how community can flourish in the presence of vulnerability. To lean on others, we must first give ourselves permission to let down our guard. This isn't always easy, especially in a world that often puts self-reliance on a pedestal, but it is essential for healing and growth. And it demonstrates that community can be found in unexpected places—whether in a crowded nightclub, a thoughtful conversation, or a shared experience of struggle.

Ultimately, the power of community lies in its ability to transform isolation into solidarity, fear into strength, and struggle into shared purpose. And equally important is recognizing that relationships are reciprocal. While some connections may be based on surface-level commonality, and they have a place, building meaningful connections requires effort and care. It requires a balance between giving and receiving within your communities. True connection isn't just about taking support when you need it; it's about being there for others when they are in need, too. Even small gestures—like checking in with someone or sending a simple "I'm thinking of you" message—can have a significant impact. These acts of compassion remind people they are not alone and often can intersect at moments of need when they don't think they are seen.

Diversity in Community and Sisterhood

> "Making the choice to diversify my network was a first critical step for me in transforming my life."
>
> —**Kelly Hoey**

Community is not a one-size-fits-all concept. Support networks take many forms, and not every relationship is designed to meet every need. By exploring the diversity within communities and sisterhoods, we can better understand how varied relationships—whether they stem from family, friendships, or professional networks—play a critical role in individual growth, empowerment, and resilience. These connections do more than provide emotional support; they help enhance our ability to navigate life's challenges with strength and confidence.

Engaging with a broad spectrum of individuals opens our minds to new perspectives, encouraging us to view the world through diverse lenses. Research supports this idea. A study conducted by researchers from Harvard Business School revealed that diversity in social interactions is directly linked to greater happiness.[2] The study analyzed data from over 51,000 individuals across the globe. Participants reported on their well-being and described the previous day's social interactions, which ranged from engaging with strangers and acquaintances to spending time with friends and family. The findings were striking: The more diverse people's social relationships, the happier they felt, regardless of the total time spent socializing or the number of interactions.

As Mindy Grossman aptly says, "Community is critical; it gives you education that supports your life stages." Whether it's helping you overcome personal challenges or advancing your growth, the connections you cultivate adapt as your needs evolve. Mindy spearheaded this when at the helm of Weight Watchers, in partnership with Oprah Winfrey, empowering women to achieve personal health goals while fostering a sense of camaraderie. The community provides more than just practical guidance on diet and exercise—it offers a safe, judgment-free environment where women can share their struggles and triumphs, encouraging one another to succeed. Members often publicly cite the bonds formed within these groups as essential to their journeys, showing how shared goals and mutual accountability help them not just make their transformations, but maintain them.

We can apply a corporate mindset to personal community building by approaching our social networks as dynamic and evolving ecosystems. In business, leaders recognize that effective networks are diverse, purpose-driven, and continually adapting to new challenges. The same principles apply to personal communities.

The community you build, become a part of, and/or support is iterative, and it changes as you change. You may have a foundational community, one that weaves in and out of your life stages alongside you. Some years you are tighter than others, but there is always a thread keeping you connected. You may have groups intersecting with your current stage of life, as they cross the same themes, hurdles, and goals. You may surround yourself with people younger than you, to keep you young at heart, connected to popular culture and how it's evolving.

The relationships you nurture should reflect your current needs while being open to change and growth. Here are some examples to consider:

- **Foundational communities:** These are the people who have been with you through multiple life stages. While the intensity of these relationships may ebb and flow over the years, they remain constant threads, offering stability and deep-rooted connection.
- **Stage-of-life communities:** These groups align with where you are now. They may address shared themes, goals, or challenges you're currently navigating, such as career growth, parenting, or retirement.
- **Growth communities:** Surrounding yourself with people who are smarter, more experienced, or more knowledgeable in areas you're curious about can fuel continuous learning. These individuals challenge you to expand your thinking and inspire personal growth.
- **Pay-it-forward communities:** Sometimes the most fulfilling connections come from giving back. Engaging in nonprofit work, volunteering, or mentoring others allows you to contribute meaningfully while building relationships rooted in generosity and service.
- **Adventure communities:** As we age, it's natural to yearn for the energy and excitement of earlier years. Joining groups that embrace adventure, creativity, or spontaneity can help you rediscover youthful joy while fostering intergenerational learning.

Support Impacts Our Health

In our journey to find communities and networks that support us, we find more than just a source of comfort—we also benefit from our mental and physical well-being. While it might seem intuitive that strong social bonds make us feel good, research has repeatedly shown that the benefits go far beyond emotional satisfaction; they have measurable effects on our health, longevity, and even resilience to disease. They support the individual mission we are each on.

One of the most well-documented psychological benefits of connection is its ability to reduce stress—a key goal we identified in Chapter 2. When we share our burdens with others—whether it's venting about a challenging day, seeking advice, or simply enjoying the presence of someone who understands—we activate the brain's reward systems. And the act of talking through our problems releases oxytocin, which not only helps us feel closer to others (after all, oxytocin is sometimes referred to as the "cuddle hormone") but also has a calming effect on the body by reducing cortisol, the hormone responsible for stress.

Studies examine how social relationships impact stress regulation. Researchers have found that individuals with strong support networks exhibit lower levels of cortisol in response to stressful events than those who were socially isolated, supporting the notion that community doesn't just feel good—it actively buffers us from the physiological toll of stress.[3]

The benefits of connection extend beyond immediate stress relief. Long-term health outcomes have also been closely tied to the quality of our social relationships. In a meta-analysis published in *PLOS Medicine* in 2010, data from 148 studies involving over 300,000 participants was analyzed. The findings showed that individuals with strong social ties had a 50% higher likelihood of survival over a given time period than those with weaker connections. To put this into perspective, the study concluded that the impact of social relationships on mortality risk was comparable to well-established health factors such as smoking cessation or maintaining a healthy weight.[4]

Physiologically, being part of a supportive community has been shown to improve heart health, enhance immune function, and even reduce chronic pain. A 2016 study in the *American Journal of Public Health* found that individuals who felt socially supported were less likely to develop hypertension, a major risk factor for heart disease. The researchers theorized that this is partly because connection helps regulate blood pressure through its calming effects on the nervous system.

Beyond physical benefits, social connection is also a critical factor in resilience and mental health. As individuals face significant life challenges, such as illness or grief, they often find that their ability to cope is strengthened by the support of others. Sisterhood, in particular, plays a unique role here, in not only emotional connection, but as a powerful source of resilience. For example, a study published in *The Journal of Clinical Oncology* in 2016 found that women with breast cancer who participated in peer-support groups reported higher quality of life and lower levels of anxiety than those who faced their diagnosis alone.[5]

What makes connection so powerful is not just the act of being with others but the sense of belonging and validation it fosters. When we feel understood and valued, we experience what psychologist Abraham Maslow described as the fulfillment of a core human need: belonging. This sense of connection is what allows communities—whether they are formed through shared life stages, professional endeavors, or sisterhoods—to become spaces where we as individuals can thrive.

The Community of Me

> "To heal forward you have to heal backwards, and the experiences you have with yourself also shape who you become."
>
> **—Alexis Thomas**

In addition to building connections with others, there lies a deep opportunity to discover and nurture what can be called the "community of me." This concept emphasizes the importance of the relationship you cultivate with yourself—a bond that is critical because it also impacts your capacity to have relationships with others. When you reflect on the question *Who is the community of me?* you open a door to exploring the unique tapestry of your lived experiences. These experiences not only define you but also offer an opportunity to deepen your self-awareness, self-love, and appreciation for the many layers that make you who you are.

Engaging with your personal community involves identifying and honoring the activities that allow you to connect with yourself on a meaningful level. For someone passionate about solo sports, "community of me" time might mean mornings spent hitting tennis balls with a machine or enjoying a serene run along the water at sunrise. For others, it could involve experimenting with new recipes while following an online influencer, immersing themselves in the creative rhythm of knitting, or simply engaging in quiet moments of reflection. These activities are not just hobbies; they are acts of self-care and self-discovery where the focus shifts inward to reconnect with one's inner world.

Interestingly, this ability to coexist with others while also embracing solo exploration is innate. If you observe children, you'll notice that they naturally embody this balance—they play alongside others but also engage in moments of self-directed play. When I watch my daughter do this, it serves as a reminder of the enriching potential of creating and nurturing the "community of me."

The idea of embracing and nurturing your inner community aligns closely with psychological theories of self-compassion, mindfulness, and personal well-being. While engaging with others fuels us, engaging in solitary, meaningful activities can also enhance self-compassion by providing space for reflection and self-care. And focused solo activities can enhance self-awareness and reduce stress because these practices help us build stronger connections to our inner selves, leading to a greater sense of contentment.[6]

Solo activities, particularly those that engage creativity or physical exertion, can induce "flow states," as identified by psychologist Mihaly Csikszentmihalyi.[7] Flow enhances happiness, engagement, and personal fulfillment by immersing individuals in the present moment. A flow state is that magical feeling when you're so deeply immersed in an activity that you lose track of time and your sense of self beyond the point of distraction. Everything around you becomes secondary, and your focus is entirely absorbed in what you're doing. Athletes often describe it as being "in the zone." Artists and musicians might say they're "lost in the moment." Even someone tackling a challenging project at work might experience this enriching sense of engagement. In this state, it's not just being productive—it's a peak state of enjoyment, creativity, and effortless focus. Flow is also cited as a key driver of creativity and innovation. Many breakthroughs, whether in art, science, or business, have come from individuals immersed in deep flow states. It's during these moments that our brains make unexpected connections, leading to fresh ideas and solutions.

Psychological principles like self-compassion, mindfulness, and flow underscore the value of our "community of me" investments. It reveals their ability to reduce stress, spark creativity, and enhance personal fulfillment. When we nurture our "community of me," we unlock the potential to live more engaged, balanced, and content lives.

Intentionality and Rewiring

> "In life-changing moments you often come to terms with realizing you don't have to be in it alone, but you do need to know what you need and what you can give. Who is good for what, and how are you good for them?"
>
> **—Trish Barillas**

In pivotal moments, life often teaches us an essential truth: You don't have to navigate challenges alone. But to truly thrive, you must know what you need, what you can give, and how to discern who is best suited to walk the journey with you. It's a matter of intentionality—understanding the dynamics of relationships and communities, and how they shape us.

As Trish Barillas states above, these are questions we must intermittently revisit. Whether you're part of a community, a network, or a sisterhood, clarity about your expectations and contributions is key. Like any meaningful relationship, thriving within these circles requires deliberate effort: choosing the right people to share your vulnerabilities with, and recognizing that not everyone is equipped to handle the same level of openness.

> "I have a tension between trust and engaging with people on a nonprofessional level."
>
> **—Anonymous**

Much like any relationship, being part of a community involves trust, mutual respect, and a give-and-take dynamic. However, entering and engaging in these spaces often requires a process of unlearning and rewiring. For example, consider how rigid expectations of what a friendship or connection "should" look like might limit your opportunities for meaningful relationships. What if we approached relationships with curiosity instead?

By broadening our perspectives, we enrich our lives. Perhaps this means saying yes to activities outside your comfort zone—attending a theater performance, trying your hand at painting, or even learning to dance. Think of life as a rich tapestry: each new experience adds vibrant threads, textures, and colors to the fabric of our existence. The key is to remain open and allow new possibilities to unfold naturally.

A Journey of Yes

When I left Wall Street in 2009, I made a personal commitment to say "yes" to exploration for six months. Yes to meeting new people, yes to trying new activities, and yes to joining spaces that piqued my curiosity. One such experience was joining a community of transcendental healers—a decision that expanded my understanding of connection and personal growth.

This group introduced me to practices and perspectives I hadn't encountered before. Their explorations included elements I wasn't prepared to embrace, such as the use of psychedelics, but their conversations left a lasting impact. Psychedelics, they explained, could facilitate profound spiritual growth and moments of "self-transcendence," where the ego dissolves, and individuals feel a deep connection to something infinite. While I wasn't inclined to experiment myself, I found value in listening to their insights.

Research supports these claims, highlighting how psychedelic therapies can help individuals confront and process emotional trauma. A growing body of evidence suggests that these substances, under guided therapeutic conditions, can induce transformative states without retraumatizing individuals.[8] For me, the experience wasn't about adopting their practices but about embracing a growth mindset—being open to perspectives that challenged my own.

Ultimately, these months of exploration underscored a vital lesson: personal growth often comes from unexpected sources. When we approach life with curiosity and intentionality, we open ourselves to insights and connections that can reshape our paths.

What serves us in our journey of life, is how we can listen, learn, adapt. When we have that mindset we are also more open to letting communities into our lives with intentionality. We also open the possibility of letting in things we didn't even know we needed, until that exposure happens. As the oft-quoted poem by Brian A. Chalker reminds us, "People come into your life for a reason, a season, or a lifetime," and that is okay. We also learn that all of us influence and are equally influenced by the networks we choose to associate with (or are born into). Our choices on who to connect with, turn to, or lean on for support have personal impacts and consequences, from the partners we choose to how we make sense of the world to the careers we pursue. All of these individual choices combine in turn to create momentum for collective growth and possibility.

As we navigate life, we must also accept the fluid nature of relationships. Not everyone we meet is meant to stay forever. The key is to recognize their value in the moment and understand how they contribute to our growth.

Our relationships influence how we see the world, the careers we pursue, and the choices we make. At the same time, we influence others in return. Together, these connections form the foundation for collective growth and progress.

Here are practical steps to cultivate intentionality and embrace the rewiring process:

- **Accept the fluidity of connections.** Relationships evolve as we move through life stages: our 20s, 30s, 40s, retirement, and beyond. Be open to these changes and adapt accordingly.
- **Identify your "911 Circle."** These are the people you can rely on in critical moments. They may not be your closest friends, but they are dependable and action-oriented when you need them most.
- **Balance human connection and digital platforms.** While digital tools provide valuable ways to connect, they shouldn't replace genuine, in-person relationships. Find meaningful ways to integrate both into your life. Tools like the Mindful Nation App can help bridge this gap by fostering intentional online interactions.

Intentionality is a practice, not a destination. By being mindful of who we invite into our lives and how we engage with them, we create opportunities for personal and collective transformation. Communities and networks shape us, often in ways we don't immediately recognize. By staying open to new experiences and perspectives, we allow ourselves to grow beyond the limits of what we thought was possible.

Life, like any rich tapestry, becomes more vibrant when we weave in diverse threads. So remain curious. Embrace the unknown. And trust that every connection, every experience, and every challenge has the potential to add depth and meaning to your personal journey.

Gut check question: "Are the vibrations of the people in your life in alignment with what you want out of your life?"

—Yvette Vargas

If our relationship with communities is an evolving process, one that relates to your desires and needs today and your aspirations in the future, then the communities you invest in need to support the expression of things you desire to achieve.

Here is an exercise to help you align purpose with where you invest your time, a guide to how you seek out like-minded people, people that align with your passions. Here are a few examples:

"I want to laugh hard."
"I want to travel more."
"I want to be a CEO one day."

- What are the experiences you want to have in the next 5 years?
- In the next 10 years?
- In the next 20?

Tying This to the Professional Mindset

Networking expert and author Kelly Hoey, whose insights are woven throughout this chapter, attributes every major milestone in her career to the power of her network. Through deep self-reflection, she came to a transformative realization: Her network consistently saw greater potential in her than she ever imagined for herself. This belief propelled her to step out of the comfort zone of a stable management career and dive into the unpredictable waters of entrepreneurship.

Kelly's network didn't just offer encouragement; they actively created opportunities. One such opportunity led her to co-found a startup accelerator, a venture she might never have dreamed of on her own. In 2015, when she felt a burning desire to write a book, it was her network that transformed this audacious dream into a reality. Reflecting on her journey, she notes, "Yes, I wrote the damn book, but my network made that effort possible!"

Kelly also humorously highlights a universal truth: "Frankly, the pivotal role of networks in our lives is why I find it so amusing when someone says they 'made it all on their own.' Besides being untrue, how dull." Her journey serves as a testament to the undeniable role networks play in shaping both our personal and professional trajectories.

For Kelly, making the choice to diversify her network was the first critical step in transforming her life, both personally and professionally. This is because typically our networks want the best for us and that "what's best" viewpoint can create conflict, especially when what's best for us in our mind is completely at odds with what our network imagines is best for us. Finding others who have explored beyond the edges we've wavered at exploring is essential.

What makes a good network is also the life skill that enables you to see the world less judgmentally: listening. Not hearing, but listening. Listen with curiosity and an openness to having the veil lifted on what you think you know (which is far more interesting than always being right).

Authenticity is also a cornerstone of meaningful networks and communities. When we approach relationships with authenticity—sharing openly and without the need for validation—we discover more about ourselves.[9] In doing so, we unintentionally invite others to join us on our journey. Further, this process of connection is not about the size of the community, whether it's one person or a thousand. Instead, it's about the quality of the bond and the motivations behind it.

Building authentic community allows us to let go of the need for approval and instead focus on genuine connection. It's through these connections that we thrive, experiencing growth in areas we may not have been able to reach on our own. Networks provide us with more than opportunities—they offer connection to health, a deeper connection to self, and access to possibilities we might not have envisioned.

When we build community and sisterhood in an authentic way, we discover more of who we are, and we inadvertently invite others to join us on our journey. We find our community when we share with our guard down versus seeking approval or validation. A community of one or a thousand—it's a pivotal switch in terms of motivations. Community and networks are how we live and thrive—connection to health, connection to self, connection to possibilities we can't see alone.

The power of professional networks lies in their ability to expose us to diverse perspectives and possibilities. By intentionally seeking out individuals who challenge our thinking, we create opportunities for growth that extend beyond the limits of our own imaginations. As Kelly Hoey's journey demonstrates, success is rarely achieved in isolation. Instead, it is built on a foundation of collaboration, mutual support, and shared vision.

When we embrace this mindset, we not only create a network of support but also contribute to the growth and success of others. In doing so, we build a life richer in connection and opportunity—one that allows us to see the world not just as it is, but as it could be.

Bust Imposter Syndrome

"You are Lisa f-cking Mateo"

—said to Lisa Mateo, business correspondent, Bloomberg

As we address the power of support, I also want to give a nod to what so many interviewed also admit that they combat: imposter syndrome. Having imposter syndrome means believing that we're not as competent as others perceive us to be. Even if external evidence clearly shows we're skilled and accomplished, imposter syndrome whispers self-doubt into our mind. It convinces us that our successes are due to luck, timing, or even deception, rather than our own capabilities or efforts.

Lisa Mateo is a correspondent at Bloomberg and, at the time of this writing, a markets reporter for its top-rated morning radio program, *Bloomberg Surveillance*. Previously, she was an anchor for CBS News Radio, the host of *Celebrity Taste Makers*, and an Emmy-nominated reporter and anchor at WPIX-TV. To say she is accomplished would be an understatement.

I have known Lisa since high school, where she stood out as an athlete, a leader, and someone admired for both her talent and her kindness. Yet, over time, she developed a habit of negative self-talk, which fed her self-doubt. This struggle was largely tied to her journey of regaining a healthy amount of weight post-pregnancy, but it also influenced how she viewed herself beyond her appearance.

After giving birth, Lisa became less active, and as the weight accumulated—50 pounds above her pre-pregnancy weight—she felt lost. Her confidence waned, and negative self-talk became a cycle that led to deeper feelings of inadequacy and even depression. The self-doubt clouded her perception of herself, making her accomplishments feel distant and undeserved.

Then one day Lisa looked in the mirror and no longer recognized the woman staring back at her. That moment became a turning point. She decided to take back control, channeling her energy into personal transformation. She founded a wellness group where people could come together, share their insecurities, exercise, and find support in a community. She also pursued eye movement desensitization and reprocessing (EMDR) therapy, which proved to be a game-changer. Through this journey, self-care became an integral part of her daily practice, and she gradually reshaped her perspective.

Today, Lisa continues to work on seeing herself in a positive light. While she has made tremendous progress, she acknowledges that giving herself credit remains an ongoing effort. The voice of self-doubt still lingers, especially as she reaches new heights in her career. Each step forward brings a new wave of questioning: *How did I get here? Am I truly worthy?* But her family, colleagues, and community help hold up a mirror, reflecting back the reality she sometimes struggles to see.

"You are Lisa f-cking Mateo," a colleague told her—a reminder to snap her out of her own negative talk and back to the reality of her accomplishments. Sometimes, when we forget our worth, the people who believe in us the most become our greatest source of strength. This phenomenon, and stories like Lisa's, are surprisingly common. People in all stages of life—students, professionals, creatives, and especially high achievers—may experience it. Ironically, imposter syndrome often disproportionately affects those who are thriving, as they begin to wonder whether their accomplishments measure up to their own or others' expectations.

Living with imposter syndrome can take a significant toll on an individual's mental and emotional well-being. It encourages self-doubt; it can make us feel the need to overcompensate by pushing ourselves to achieve perfection; it can lead us to dread seeking out opportunities because we believe we aren't good enough and we fear both failure and success.

An effective way to silence the voice of self-doubt is by building or joining supportive communities like DealMakeHers, Luminary, and the Wie Suite—communities that foster both personal and collective growth. They enable us to surround ourselves with supportive individuals (whether they're peers, mentors, or colleagues), giving us encouragement and the validation we struggle to give ourselves. And sometimes imposter syndrome convinces us to downplay our achievements, but a strong community not only celebrates our successes with us but helps us recognize them as well-earned. And when we forget our worth, they remind us: *You are more than enough. You belong. You earned this.*

For the second exercise in this chapter let's take stock: *How do you identify the source for the result for the problem, challenge, moment you are facing?*

Sometimes tapping the wrong networks can inadvertently hold you back. They can clip your wings or provide support for the wrong the problem. You may have outgrown them or maybe the support you tapped is so emotionally protective of you, with their own unconscious bias, they can't serve you in certain moments of need.

Ask yourself: What is going on with me right now?

- Do I need nourishment?
- Do I need motivation?
- Do I need guidance?
- Do I need to be challenged?
- Do I need help with my blind spots?

Based on the responses, ask next: Who do I need to tap to get what I need?

Climb and Lift

While we learn and grow as individuals, benefiting from the power of community, it's also critical to remember that the opportunity of growth isn't only on your way up, but also in our ability to help others rise.

The philosophy of "climb and lift" emphasizes a dual responsibility: striving for personal growth and success while simultaneously creating opportunities for others to rise alongside you. This approach highlights the importance of giving back, sharing insights gained through lived experiences, and using one's achievements as a platform to uplift others.

My mother (introduced in Chapter 5), has been a believer and practitioner of the climb-and-lift mentality throughout her career. Today, as an executive coach, she leans into her opportunity to give back by listening to understand other's fears, anxieties, or reservations and works with her clients to level set. Through her own personal and professional journeys, she helps them overcome their roadblocks and find their sense of confidence and belonging. And it's an interesting two-way growth journey; as she helps others unlock their potential, she too continues to grow through new conversations and challenges. While success is often seen as a solitary climb, climb and lift shifts the focus toward collective progress.

When we strive to grow and succeed, we often lean on the power of community—the collective wisdom, support, and encouragement of those around us. However, true growth is not solely about climbing upward. It's also about reaching back and lifting others along the way. Growth is amplified when we share the lessons we've learned, open doors for others, and use our experiences to support those who may benefit from our guidance.

Climb and lift aligns with leadership principles rooted in mentorship and servant leadership. Leaders who adopt this mindset not only achieve personal success but also cultivate inclusive environments where others can thrive. Furthermore, the act of lifting others often extends far beyond the initial interaction. When you support someone, you are more likely to pass that encouragement along to others, creating a ripple effect within your community or organization. This collective uplift fosters collaboration and empowerment, where individuals become more motivated to help each other succeed. Over time, these ripples can grow into a powerful wave of positive change, strengthening bonds and driving a shared commitment to progress.

Helping others accelerates our own growth. Teaching a concept or offering advice requires us to articulate our understanding, which deepens our own knowledge. And supporting someone else along their journey gives us the opportunity to see challenges from a new perspective, which enhances our adaptability and problem-solving skills. In giving, we gain—a truth that reinforces the value of the climb-and-lift approach.

Growth isn't just about reaching the top; it's about creating pathways for others to follow. When leaders embrace the climb-and-lift philosophy, they cultivate an environment where success is shared, growth is amplified, and the journey becomes as meaningful as the destination.

In totality, the power of community and sisterhood illustrates that our true strength is found in the connections that we weave with one another. It also accentuates that community is a living, breathing network where every shared experience—whether moments of triumph or instances of vulnerability—adds depth and resilience to our collective spirit. By embracing both the individual uniqueness and the common aspects we all share, we learn that every story, every challenge, and every success contributes to our greater whole. And through genuine connection, we can harness the collective wisdom and strength of our communities to overcome adversity, foster personal growth, and create a nurturing environment that enhances our lives.

Chapter 6 Contributors:

Mindy Grossman, Trish Barillas, Alexis Thomas, Yvette Vargas, Clarissa Ramos-Cafarelli, Mina Fader, Lolita Lopez, Cate Luzio, Jennifer Gootman, Alice Kim, Kelly Hoey, Lisa Mateo

7

Normalizing Slow

Reclaiming Balance and the Art of Pacing Yourself

In a constantly connected world, transitioning from a FOMO mentality to a "love of where I'm at" mode is no easy feat. It takes a level of self-content and requires the ability to embrace the power of being present.

So far we have explored the journey to purpose, the importance of self-compassion, and the strength we can gain from community. A recurring theme in this exploration is the balance between healthy solitude and social engagement—understanding when interactions uplift us and when they begin to deplete us. Finding this equilibrium requires self-reflection and a conscious effort to prioritize what truly serves our well-being.

In looking at the benefits we gain from normalizing slow, let's look at the relationship between FOMO (also known as Fear of Missing Out) and JOMO (Joy of Missing Out).

Often fueled by social media, FOMO encourages constant comparison, leading to feelings of inadequacy, anxiety, and low self-esteem. The pressure to stay connected and involved can drive compulsive behaviors—overbooking schedules, making impulsive decisions, and prioritizing quantity over quality in relationships. Ironically, this pursuit of connection often results in isolation, as we become more focused on what we might be missing rather than fully engaging in the present. Studies have linked FOMO to increased anxiety, stress, and difficulty making decisions, ultimately preventing us from experiencing true contentment and inhibiting us from enjoying the present moment, the true point of satisfaction.

> "Those who regularly engage in being present with aesthetically pleasing environments exhibit lower levels of anxiety and higher levels of improved cognition."
>
> **—Jennifer Walsh, founder of the Lost Art of Being Human**

In recent years, JOMO has emerged as a powerful countertrend, emphasizing intentional disconnection, mindfulness, and contentment with a slower, simpler way of living. JOMO encourages less comparison, less self-imposed pressure to say yes to everything, and less negative self-talk. Unlike FOMO, which thrives on anxiety and social comparison, JOMO is rooted in self-awareness, solitude, and the fulfillment found in intentional living.

A 2024 qualitative study by Pabon and colleagues found that millennials who actively practice JOMO report greater self-awareness, reduced anxiety, and improved relationships.[1] Key themes from the study highlight the benefits of setting digital boundaries, engaging in offline hobbies, and fostering deeper, more meaningful connections. The findings also suggest that mindful disengagement from social pressures leads to a sense of fulfillment rather than emptiness. Participants in the study reported improved focus, reduced stress, and better emotional regulation.

Similarly, research by Rautela and Sharma found that individuals who embrace JOMO tend to engage in reflective and mindful practices such as journaling, nature walks, and reading.[2] These activities contribute to a more balanced and fulfilling life, reinforcing the idea that slowing down enhances well-being.

Transitioning from FOMO to JOMO is ultimately about redefining what we consider success—not as a relentless pursuit of activity but as a state of intentionality, presence, and balance. In a culture that glorifies busyness, it can be difficult to trust that we are enough as we are. Many people reach a breaking point, overwhelmed by the pressure to keep up, only to find peace in slowing down.

Numerous studies[3] also show us that chasing constant stimulation leads to burnout, stress, and reduced overall well-being. However, when we embrace a slower, more intentional approach to life, we can cultivate deeper connections, improve mental clarity, and reduce this draining pressure to always be "in the know," to be everywhere and everything.

Normalizing slow(er) living allows for recalibration in a hyper-connected, always connected world, and it gives us a point of view with greater appreciation of everyday moments, fostering a sense of gratitude and well-being. By embracing slower living, we give ourselves empowerment to set healthier boundaries, prioritize real-life experiences over external validation, and cultivate a healthier and more fulfilling lifestyle. The key lies in trusting that true, sustainable happiness is not found in the endless pursuit of experiences but in the quality and intentionality of those experiences.

JOMO or normalizing slow does not mean rejecting social life altogether either. Instead, it is about choosing when and how to engage, ensuring that interactions align with our personal values and well-being.

In this chapter we will explore, through stories of others, ways to embrace slow while still living a life fulfilled.

The Power of No

Earlier in her career, Stacy Berns, owner of Berns Communications Group—a leading public relations firm in the retail and consumer space and the founder of three retail influencer networks, including DealMakeHers and the Z-Suite—renowned for crafting compelling brand narratives, fostering strategic partnerships, and building executive thought leadership platforms—learned a critical lesson about setting boundaries and the power of saying no.

As a high-flying public relations professional, Stacy thrived on her fast-paced lifestyle. She traveled constantly, meeting clients, attending events, and ensuring her presence was seen in all the right places. Her dedication and relentless drive were key to her success, but they also came at a cost. And her "always-on" approach to work was tested when she experienced a health crisis that forced her to reevaluate her priorities.

One winter day, Stacy flew to Chicago for a handful of meetings. In a taxi ride on the way to her second meeting she felt an unusual pain in her arms. As she neared her destination, she also began sweating and found it increasingly difficult to breathe. Sensing something was seriously wrong, she called the journalist she was scheduled to meet, Bethany McLean of *Vanity Fair*, and told her, "You need to come outside to meet me." Before Bethany could reach her, Stacy collapsed in the snow-filled street outside the restaurant, surrounded by strangers. Initially diagnosed with a heart attack, she spent eight days in the ICU at Northwestern Hospital.

Doctors later determined that Stacy had suffered from vasovagal syncope, a condition in which the body's normal ability to regulate blood pressure temporarily malfunctions. This leads to a sudden drop in heart rate and blood pressure, causing fainting episodes. According to the Cleveland Clinic, approximately one in three people may experience vasovagal syncope at least once in their lifetime.[4] While not typically life-threatening, this condition is often triggered by stress, anxiety, extreme fatigue, or physical exhaustion—all of which were routine elements of Stacy's work-driven life.

What she learned: *You cannot spread yourself so thin it's at the expense of your own health.* This health scare was a wake-up call. Stacy realized that pushing herself to the brink of exhaustion was unsustainable and unhealthy. More importantly, she learned that her ability to say no—to excessive demands, relentless travel, and the expectation to be everywhere at once—was not just beneficial but necessary for her well-being.

Today if you follow Stacy online, you still see a dynamic, multitasking businesswoman, but behind the curtain she maintains her stamina through boundaries she has established that allow her to have healthier balances. While socializing is integral to her profession, she chooses not to drink at work events, allowing her to remain clear-headed and energized. She skips the after-parties and recognizes that networking doesn't have to extend into the late hours, and she prioritizes rest over staying out just for the sake of appearances. She carves out vacations and PTO days in between heavy work engagements to recharge the battery. And she gives herself permission to decline opportunities that do not align with her well-being or long-term objectives. What she says no to is fluid, adjusting as her needs evolve.

For many professionals, especially those in high-stakes industries, saying no can feel counterintuitive. The pressure to be available, to take every opportunity, and to constantly prove one's value can feel like setting boundaries is failing to deliver. However, Stacy's experience demonstrates the reality that setting limits is not a sign of weakness—it's a demonstration of self-respect and long-term strategic thinking.

The power to say no allows us to prioritize what truly matters. When every request is met with an automatic yes, energy and focus become diluted, leading to burnout. Instead, carefully selecting commitments ensures that time and effort are invested in endeavors that align with personal values and professional goals. Stacy has learned to embrace this philosophy, recognizing that success isn't defined by how much one does but by how effectively one operates. Saying no is not about shutting doors—it's about making intentional choices that protect our energy, health, and peace of mind. In accepting this we learn to understand that boundaries are not barriers; they are safeguards that allow us to show up as our best selves in both professional and personal spaces.

For our first chapter exercise, here are some practical steps you can take to embrace the practice of normalizing slow(er):

- **Redefine success.** Check back with your purpose journey work from Chapter 4. Shift your focus from external achievements to internal well-being. What activities support your priorities and personal values in ways that bring joy and fulfillment?
- **Simplify your schedule.** Prioritize fewer, more meaningful commitments rather than overloading your calendar. What is one thing a month you can say no to, for the next three months?
- **Engage in slow activities.** Select one hobby or offline activity to support your sense of presence and fuel personal growth, satisfaction, and commitment to it for the next three months.

The Opportunity of Nature's Connection

"Quieting our soul is necessary work."

—Jennifer Walsh, founder of Lost Art of Being Human and author of *Walk Your Way Calm*

Sometimes when we are running and running, living in a relentless cycle of "always doing," it can be increasingly difficult to find ourselves in the noise. And it's in the quieting of our soul that we find the avenues that help us thrive.

As explored in Chapter 2, the human brain is not designed to function at full capacity without pause for endless durations, because our processing capabilities will become depleted. Just as muscles rebuild after exercise, our cognitive abilities strengthen when we allow moments of quiet. Neuroscience confirms that the brain is not designed for relentless processing; instead, it requires downtime to consolidate learning, strengthen memory, and enhance our problem-solving skills.[5]

In her early 30s, Jennifer Walsh was an energetic entrepreneur, the visionary founder of Beauty Bar, the first omni-channel beauty brand in the United States (founded in in 1998). She changed the way people shopped for beauty and wellness by allowing shoppers to see and experience niche and independent beauty products in her brick-and-mortar stores, on her e-commerce website, and her weekly TV show. It was a first to market fully interactive experience in an open sell environment. Beauty Bar was acquired in 2010 by Quidsi, the same year Quidsi was acquired by Amazon.

Throughout this journey, Jennifer lived in a constant state of high intensity, driven by the belief that pushing herself to the limit was proof of success. Living every day "hard core to the max," as she described it, she prided herself on being the first in the office, never taking a day off, and always striving to prove her worth through relentless effort. To her, this lifestyle represented success and achievement.

That perception changed when she began experiencing bowel irregularities and pains she could not ignore. Initially resistant to medical intervention, she eventually sought help, only to receive a stop-her-in-her-tracks diagnosis: a tumor the size of a grapefruit in her colon. Misdiagnosed the night before surgery as metastatic cancer, she was stricken with an overwhelming feeling of fear and uncertainty.

Major surgery followed, a significant part of her colon was removed, and her recovery spanned nearly a year. Today Jennifer jokes about her long-lasting post-surgery nickname, Semicolon. She struggled so much to reprogram herself to slow down that her surgeon had to intervene to prevent her from returning to work prematurely, clear evidence of her unhealthy ingrained habit of equating productivity with self-worth.

It was a wake-up call that taught her she didn't have to do all she did to prove herself, that seeking external validation would never be fulfilling prophecy and would never give her solace. She also realized that it's hard to shut off an Alpha brain (going back to our personal PIs), but she did have the capacity to rechannel that energy in healthier ways. She could find other avenues to fuel soul and purpose to be an impact person in new ways.

Today, Jennifer Walsh is an esteemed author, consultant, and faculty advisor to institutions such as the Brain Health Initiative at Harvard and the University of Pennsylvania's Center for Neuroaesthetics. Her work sits at the intersection of beauty, retail, nature, and neuroaesthetics. She passionately explores the ways in which our deep-rooted connection to nature influences our overall well-being. Tapping into the curiosity about how nature affects our well-being that she has always held, she now spends time with neuroscientists around the country to study this link to nature and its effects on the brain.[6]

In her work, Jennifer also studies the innate connection between humans, beauty, and nature, with an emphasis that our subconscious is always talking to us and we just need to listen.[7] When we listen, we start to notice small but impactful things throughout the day that make us feel good, unconsciously helping us navigate through life's challenges. She taps into this knowledge with the concept of "microdosing on noticing"—the practice of consciously identifying the little things that bring us delight throughout the day. This could be as simple as the warmth of the sun on our skin, the rhythmic sound of leaves rustling, or the scent of fresh air after rainfall. Over time, this practice rewires our brain to seek out beauty and positivity, helping to counterbalance stress and uncertainty.

Jennifer's work illustrates that mindful breaks, daydreaming, and even short walks in nature can help reset cognitive function, much like sleep does for memory consolidation. And this is why time in nature and the integration of biophilic elements in everyday life can have transformative impact. Spaces, textures, and colors speak to our inner selves. For example, wood has long provided shelter and warmth. For centuries, humas have turned to it for cooking, for heating, even back when we were hunters and gatherers. Similar correlations can be made by the significance of natural light and fresh air in our lives. Understanding and incorporating these elements into daily life can contribute to optimal health and longevity.

Seeking Awe in Everyday Moments

By stepping away from the noise of constant "doing," we create space for deeper insights and mental clarity, fostering resilience and well-being. But this will require individualized approaches to understanding our personal preferences and requirements for comfort and happiness.

Seeking "awe moments"—instances of profound appreciation and wonder in everyday life—and relishing them helps signify the importance of noticing small things throughout the day that make us feel good. It helps us navigate through life's challenges. Leaning on Jennifer's approach of microdosing, we can each begin to notice and home in on the things that cultivate our awe moments. And in these moments we can reduce stress and increase positive emotions.

The worksheets in the appendix will guide you through exercises designed to identify your unique "cheat sheet" of awe interventions. These personalized strategies will serve as tools to cut through the noise, reset mental clarity, and reconnect with what truly brings us fulfillment.

Introspection as an Avenue to Slowing Down

> "I am now in the flow: intuition, introspection, yoga, and breathwork."
>
> —**Shirley Ramos Roseman**

Each day we take some 20,000 breaths, about 7.5 million breaths each year.[8] *How many do you remember?* This vital activity in our lives is often overlooked because we are moving too fast. We move unconsciously, without honoring the strength in what keeps us fundamentally alive, and we don't prioritize the stillness and discernment possible in the calm of introspective thought and activity.

Recall Shirley Ramos Roseman, introduced in Chapter 1, whose life's perspective changed at the age of 29 when she had a stroke. Throughout her journey of recovery and evolution she found an introspective alignment with the universe in a way she never imagined. Her near-death experience led her to see the world through a different lens—a lens that sought a love, not just any love but a deeper healthier love that resonated with her soul. As she became a mother she stumbled upon a quote by the Dalai Lama that would guide her shift in perspective: "If every 8-year-old in the world is taught meditation, we will eliminate violence from the world within one generation." It struck a chord with her. This mission led her to co-found BEEM—nurturing one's nature through calm, introspection, and intuition. Through its app, events, and workshops, BEEM brings mini mindfulness moments into the daily lives of children, parents, and caretakers alike.

At its core, introspection is the conscious process of looking inward, evaluating one's thoughts, emotions, and behaviors. This practice allows individuals to gain deeper self-awareness and find inner harmony, leading to improved decision-making and emotional stability. In adolescence this practice is somewhat unconscious. Studies emphasize the role of introspection in emotional regulation, particularly in adolescents, finding that individuals who engage in self-reflection develop greater control over their emotions and stress responses. As we grow older, it becomes a practice we need to be more deliberate about.

> "For me, meditation in the morning allows me to process what is sitting on my chest, move it, and reset into a place of grounding and peace."
>
> **—Khirma Eliazov, founder of Kika**

For some it's about carving out time, like early mornings, which is a common habit of successful leaders. For others it may happen at the end of the day before going to bed. What's key is incorporating it as an important, dedicated practice.

In an era defined by distractions and constant external stimuli, introspection—turning inward to examine one's thoughts and emotions—is a powerful tool for mental wellness.

Research presented in 2024 by Pandey and Yadav highlights how introspection plays a crucial role in emotional regulation, particularly in adolescents.[9] Their study found that individuals who actively reflect on their thoughts and emotions develop a better understanding of their internal experiences, leading to improved emotional control and overall mental health. Beyond emotional regulation, introspection can also enhance our resilience. It helps us find pause in the moment and access our brain's default mode network (DMN)—the neural system responsible for self-referential thinking and emotional processing.

Introspection and Effective Leadership Practices

> "As ambitious women, we always feel the need to see around the corner, constantly anticipating what is next and it is f-cking exhausting. What if we saw that differently?"
>
> **—Sheena Butler-Young, fashion business journalist**

Leadership is often associated with strategic thinking, decision-making, and inspiring teams. However, an often overlooked yet critical aspect of effective leadership is the work of introspection—the ability to slow down, pause, self-reflect, assess one's strengths and weaknesses, and develop emotional intelligence. Introspection not only fosters mental wellness but also equips leaders with the self-awareness necessary for success.[10]

In the book *Human First, Leader Second: How Self-Compassion Outperforms Self-Criticism*, Massimo Backus explores how introspection, when coupled with self-compassion, creates more resilient leaders. He argues that leaders who take time to reflect on their experiences, rather than harshly judging themselves, develop healthier coping mechanisms and a more positive leadership style.[11]

Successful leaders do not merely rely on instinct; they actively engage in self-reflection and growth-oriented practices. Leaders like Bill Gates and Oprah Winfrey advocate for the habit of reflective journaling to evaluate past decisions and refine leadership strategies. Scheduling intentional time for reflection away from the daily hustle allows us to process experiences, learn from failures, and strategize for the future. Others also recognize that introspection does not happen in isolation; allowing in feedback is a critical component to reflection. The most effective leaders seek honest input from mentors, colleagues, and subordinates to help identify blind spots and foster humility. And introspection and mindfulness go hand in hand with mindfulness practices, such as meditation and focused deep breathing, enhancing our self-awareness and emotional regulation, creating space and calm to reflect on experiences both positive and difficult and ask a growth mindset–oriented question: *What can I learn from this?*

Introspection is not a passive process—it is an active, intentional practice that elevates personal growth, our leadership effectiveness and our mental wellness. It's embracing the slow, pausing, and integrating self-reflection techniques that enhance our emotional intelligence and decision-making abilities.

Here is our second exercise for this chapter: Bringing Introspection and Breathwork into Daily Life:

- **Journaling as a guided reflection:** Capture thoughts, emotions, and reflections to track stressors. Build upon the exercise in Chapter 5. "What challenges did I face today, what did I learn from those moments?"
- **Breathwork:** Make space for simple practices like diaphragmatic breathing and box breathing activate the parasympathetic nervous system, reducing stress. Challenge yourself to try this five minutes a day for a week and reflect on how you feel.
- **Mindful walks:** Walk while focusing on your breath and how surroundings enhance your mental clarity. Take note of how you feel before focused breath and measure it against how you feel after. Note any differences.

Chapter 7 Contributors:

Stacy Berns, Jennifer Walsh, Shirley Ramos Roseman, Antonia Saint Dunbar, Kelly Hoey, Trish Barillas, Khirma Eliazov, Atoya Burleson, Sheena Butler-Young

8

Facing PTSD

Understanding and Addressing the Hidden Wounds of Past Experiences and Trauma

At the time of my medical emergency, everything escalated so quickly that I went into transaction mode, something I believe most women do as second nature. We just "get shit done."

I was tunnel-vision-focused on ensuring I could understand everything the team of doctors was telling me (as best I could while on extremely strong pain medications while still in significant discomfort). I digested and processed information so quickly, it was like drinking water out of a firehouse, and it felt like in the blink of an eye I had gone from waking up in the middle of the night to being carried out of my hotel room to lying on the floor in the ER to being attached to an epidural for surgery.

I remember the fear of thinking, "What will they open up and see? What is causing this? Will there be some big mass and the message that I don't have much time to live?" A lot runs through the mind in a moment that stops you in your tracks, but I suppressed it all, held in my tears, made my round of calls to my husband and parents, and forged ahead. I went into a five-and-a-half-hour emergency surgery and I "made it to the other side." I shed some tears from the physical difficulty of recovery—like my veins being exhausted from the IV or my legs being sore from not being able to walk, but I had never really let out the emotional tears I was holding in so tightly as I went through my trauma.

Fast-forward to being back home, when I was taken back to the hospital for potential blood clots, and it was the first time I understood the debilitating feelings caused by flashbacks, vivid imagery of my stomach being completely opened, uncontrollable shivering and tears, and thoughts on loop about what I had experienced.

Thus far throughout this book, we have explored the tools and opportunities to help us evolve and grow. We have looked at the core elements of our purpose, the key attributes that drive us, giving ourselves grace and, in the previous chapter, normalizing slow. And the reality is, as we move forward in life, there will always be triggers, and if not effectively recognized and addressed, those triggers can set us backward.

Post-traumatic stress disorder (PTSD) is a mental health condition triggered by experiencing or witnessing a traumatic event. It affects both mental wellness and physical health, and disrupts daily life and well-being. Most commonly, it can stem from experiences such as military combat, natural disasters, personal assaults, or severe accidents.[1] However, it can occur in any of us with varying degrees of impact and debilitation.

In this chapter we will examine the causes of PTSD and its impacts on mental wellness. Through stories from women interviewed and through scientific studies, we'll gain insights on how to turn what can feel like debilitating moments into opportunities to pause and learn, find gratitude, and come around stronger and more adaptable.

PTSD and Mental Wellness

> "If I know a situation will be stressful or triggering, I proactively take space. I have learned not to exacerbate a situation and further trigger my nervous system."
>
> —**Joelle Oliver**

PTSD alters brain function and body responses, causing individuals to relive trauma, avoid reminders, and experience a heightened stress response. Symptoms can include intrusive flashbacks (like I experienced when I returned to the hospital for possible blood clots), avoidance behaviors, and/or hyperarousal—linking to overactivity in the stress response system and changes in cortisol regulation.[2] (Recall from our discussion in Chapter 2 that cortisol is a key hormone tied to mental well-being.)

Avoidance can manifest in various forms, such as steering clear of places, people, or conversations that remind individuals of past trauma. Studies illustrate that avoidance is a core symptom of PTSD, often exacerbating emotional distress by reinforcing fear responses instead of allowing healing. As in my example, when individuals experience trauma, the brain links certain places, people, or situations to the original danger. To protect ourselves, we learn to avoid anything that triggers those memories. While in the moment we perceive it as a defense mechanism, it also serves as a barrier to our healing. In our avoidance, we unconsciously reinforce the idea that these situations are dangerous, preventing the brain from properly processing the trauma. Over time, studies[3] show that avoidance behaviors can worsen emotional distress by keeping individuals trapped in a cycle of fear and hypervigilance. And avoidance in PTSD is linked to increased anxiety, depression, and emotional numbing, making recovery more difficult.

In a hyperarousal state—a state of heightened psychological and physiological tension—the body's fight-or-flight system remains overactive long after a traumatic event, making a person feel constantly on edge or unsafe. It can manifest in numerous ways, such as intrusive thoughts, irritability, rapid heartbeat, emotional avoidance, muscle tension, sweating, and trembling. It can also lead to sleep disorders and fatigue, and/or persistent sadness.[4] Not all moments will be long sustaining; I was able to work through it in real time by recognizing why I was emotionally impacted and allowing myself to go through the process recognizing my trauma, honoring it, and working through it. But for some it's a chronic battle.

The good news is that there are tools and methods we can use to readjust and manage in moments that feel like setbacks to our progress. From therapeutic approaches such as cognitive behavioral therapy

(CBT) or eye movement desensitization and reprocessing (EMDR), to self-care such as mediation and breathwork, to support networks to healthy lifestyle choices, we have support options.

Finding Silver Linings Through Personal Trauma

> "I have to tell people they have cancer all the time. As a cancer survivor myself, it's a whole new level of empathy I have acquired."
>
> **—Dr. Meg Hainer, ob-gyn**

Dr. Meg Hainer has always approached life with an unwavering commitment to progress—both personally and professionally. An established obstetrician-gynecologist with over 20 years of experience, she has dedicated her career to women's health. Her practice encompasses a wide range of services, including routine gynecological care, prenatal support, and advanced reproductive health services. Known for her compassionate and patient-centered approach, she has built a reputation for truly listening to and advocating for her patients. As a patient of Dr. Hainer myself, I can personally attest to the warmth and dedication she brings to her work.

In 2022, however, Dr. Hainer found herself on the other side of the doctor-patient relationship when she was diagnosed with breast cancer. The transition from caregiver to patient was deeply jarring. She was forced to temporarily step back from her profession to endure the arduous path of cancer treatment, which included chemotherapy, surgery, radiation, and ultimately a mastectomy. Facing this battle during perimenopause added an additional layer of complexity, as the physical and emotional toll of both conditions intertwined, affecting her self-image, self-worth, and overall well-being.

The psychological impact of her diagnosis was significant. Losing her breasts, experiencing physical discomfort, and coping with vaginal pain became daily challenges—all of which was compounded by a constant, lingering fear of her cancer returning. And as an ob-gyn, she found that her professional life presented unique challenges in coping with her own trauma. The medical world she once navigated with authority and confidence became a source of trauma and emotional distress.

> "I tell someone once or twice a week they have cancer. As a physician, you have to separate emotion from the job, but as someone in remission, you are still going to have a human response."
>
> **—Dr. Meg Hainer**

Every examination, every scan, and every medical conversation has the potential to trigger anxiety and reawaken the fear that had settled within her. Her human response is what made Dr. Hainer an even more empathetic physician. She now tells her patients, "I have been on this journey too, and we are going to do this together." Her personal experience has deepened her ability to connect with those she treats, allowing her to offer not just medical advice but also heartfelt understanding. However, the weight of her experiences means that some moments still take an emotional toll. When a patient does not recover, it can trigger an emotional setback, exacerbating the PTSD she has faced since her own diagnosis.

In some ways her help of others is healing and gives her the gift of seeing life with deeper empathy. But in some instances, delivering the news or seeing a patient who doesn't recover can be a significantly debilitating moment of PTSD.

Dr. Hainer is a resilient force, however. She meets you with her smile, laughter, and fast-talking wit. And to find her own ways to cope and thrive despite her challenges, she has repositioned her mind from always "wondering what's next" to embracing the now, no longer saying, "I will do that one day," and instead doing the things she knows will make her happy, today.

> "One thing I always wanted was to have baby chickens, and now I have pet chickens, and they are my girls, and I love them."
>
> **—Dr. Meg Hainer**

One of those happy-today things for Meg are her chickens, "her girls," as she calls them. Not chickens she plans to eat, but girls she hangs with. They sit on her lap, her shoulder, they are her happy place. They serve as simple, everyday reminders of what is good in life, becoming a grounding force during difficult times. And to navigate the emotional triggers that arise from her past experiences, Dr. Hainer has incorporated positive affirmations into her daily life. She reminds herself that she was fortunate her cancer was caught early, and while she endured a difficult year, she emerged with newfound freedoms. She finds the positive side of things, such as no longer needing to wear a bra or having to undergo routine mammograms. Her hair, once lost to chemotherapy, has grown back thicker and curlier than before, and she cherishes it as a symbol of resilience. Above all, she holds gratitude for what she still has: her husband, her children, and her chickens!

Dr. Hainer's journey exemplifies the intricate relationship between trauma and resilience. Her process demonstrates the opportunity that healing is not just about surviving cancer but about rediscovering life with a renewed sense of purpose and about reclaiming the things that bring genuine joy. And for Meg Hainer, it has opened her eyes to see the silver lining in things.

The Psychological Significance of "Finding the Silver Linings"

Finding the silver lining doesn't mean denying pain or pretending that bad situations are good. Instead, it involves accepting hardship while recognizing potential growth and hidden opportunities that come with that hardship. For example, experiencing a health challenge may inspire greater appreciation for strong social connections or experiencing a breakup could foster self-reflection and a deeper appreciation for one's personal needs.

"Finding the silver linings" is a mindset and an ability to identify what enables us to thrive. Studies have shown that people who practice cognitive reframing—interpreting negative events in a constructive manner—tend to have greater ability to withstand or recover quickly from difficult conditions and have higher overall well-being. According to a study by B.L. Fredrickson[5] on the broaden-and-build theory of positive emotions, positive thinking can expand our cognitive and behavioral responses to challenges, leading to personal growth and emotional healing.[6] This perspective can reduce stress and anxiety through the positive interpretation of challenges, thus lessening emotional distress signals. It can enhance our emotional regulation skills and improve our relationships with empathy (as demonstrated by Dr. Hainer) and thus helps us develop a deeper sense of gratitude, which leads to higher levels of happiness and stronger interpersonal relationship skills. And by acknowledging the lessons learned from difficult situations, individuals develop a stronger sense of self-worth and inner strength and treat themselves more kindly during hardships rather than engaging in self-criticism—thus experiencing better psychological outcomes, including lower levels of anxiety and chance of depression.[7]

When Anxiety Is Catastrophic Thinking

Anxiety is a natural response to uncertainty. As discussed in Chapters 2 and 4, each of us has a different threshold for navigating the unknown. While moderate anxiety can be beneficial—helping us prepare, stay alert, and problem-solve—it can become overwhelming when it transforms into *catastrophic thinking*. This cognitive distortion leads individuals to expect the worst possible outcome in a given situation, even when there is little or no evidence to support such fears. By magnifying perceived threats and fostering a sense of helplessness, catastrophic thinking intensifies anxiety and contributes to unnecessary distress.

> "Now I think I am a cardiologist. Anytime my heart rate goes up, I would go into panic mode. I began to invest in MDVIP [a membership network of primary care doctors focused on personalized healthcare and wellness] and it's worth every penny."
>
> **—Jill Katz, founder of Assemble HR Consulting**

For example, imagine waiting for medical test results. A person prone to catastrophic thinking might immediately assume the worst—that the results will reveal a serious or even deadly illness—despite having no concrete reason to believe so. Or in the workplace, someone might assume one mistake will lead to reprimand and a surefire path to job termination, versus trusting it will be met with support and conversation. Over time, these thought patterns create a cycle of fear and stress, reinforcing an unsubstantiated belief that disaster is imminent. If past trauma is involved, catastrophic thinking can escalate even more quickly, as the mind becomes conditioned to anticipate danger based on previous experiences.

The danger in this, especially when associated with past traumatic experience(s) and triggers, is that catastrophic thinking amplifies symptoms of health anxiety, contributing to panic attacks and excessive worry about bodily sensations.[8] And when catastrophic thinking becomes habitual, it can have significant consequences on mental and physical well-being. This is because the brain interprets imagined threats as real, triggering the body's stress response, as explored in Chapter 2. Elevated cortisol levels, rapid heart rate, and difficulty concentrating can all stem from the persistent fear of worst-case scenarios.

Overcoming catastrophic thinking is possible. One of the most effective ways to manage it is through cognitive restructuring, a technique that helps individuals challenge irrational thoughts and replace them with more balanced perspectives. By identifying cognitive distortions and actively reframing them, individuals can break the cycle of negative thought patterns and reduce anxiety.

Trish Barillas (whom we met in Chapters 4 and 6) spoke about her approach to prepping for big moments that are often met with anxiety. She offers a structured approach.[9]

Here is a summary of her action steps to take:

- **Acknowledge the thought.** Suppressing anxious thoughts can give them more power. Instead, recognize and name the catastrophic thought as it arises. Identifying it is the first step in taking control.
- **Embrace it and don't judge it.** Avoid self-criticism. Accepting that these thoughts exist without assigning shame or blame allows for a more neutral approach to managing them.
- **Engage with your tool kit.** Implement small but effective coping strategies. This could be something tactile, like brushing your hair while focusing on each stroke, engaging in a creative activity like coloring, or calling a trusted friend for support. (Later in this chapter, we will further explore how to build a personalized anxiety-management toolkit.)

- **Stick to the facts.** Resist the urge to catastrophize by evaluating the situation objectively. Ask yourself, "What evidence supports my fear? What is the most likely outcome based on past experiences and logic?" Shifting the focus to facts rather than assumptions helps prevent rumination.
- **Engage in a mentally active task.** Shift your mind from spiraling thoughts by engaging in an activity that requires cognitive focus, such as solving a puzzle, writing in a journal, or practicing deep breathing exercises. This shift encourages problem-solving rather than dwelling on distressing possibilities.
- **Reframe and replace irrational thoughts.** Challenge exaggerated fears by consciously replacing them with more balanced perspectives. For example, instead of thinking, "I will definitely fail this assignment, and everyone will judge me," reframe your mindset to "I've prepared for this presentation, and my manager and team are there to support me and help me grow."

While it may not be possible to eliminate anxious thoughts entirely, developing healthier ways to process uncertainty can significantly improve emotional well-being and disarm moments of catastrophic thinking. By using techniques like cognitive restructuring and implementing practical coping strategies, we can regain control over thought patterns that lead to debilitation and cultivate empowerment in the face of challenges, whether big or small.

Living Less Attached to Outcomes

PTSD can often trap individuals in a cycle of fear, self-judgment, and emotional burden. One way to break free from this cycle is to adopt a mindset that is less attached to specific outcomes. When we place excessive emphasis on achieving certain results, we unintentionally add another layer of pressure to our existing trauma. This attachment to external validation and rigid expectations can hinder growth, making it difficult to fully engage in the healing process. However, by shifting toward a mindset that embraces successes and setbacks as integral parts of a broader journey, we can foster adaptability and personal transformation.

Instead of focusing on perceived shortcomings in our progress, we can shift our mindset to recognize and appreciate both the losses and the gains along the way. Acknowledging "I am still here, and I have become more dimensional because of it" reinforces the idea that personal growth is not linear. The experiences that shape us—both positive and challenging—provide valuable insights that prepare us for the next chapter of our journey. Individuals who adopt this broader perspective often develop greater emotional depth, empathy, and inner strength.

For example, as I reflect on my own recovery, I recall my surgeon's firm advice: "Melissa, this *will* be a process, and it will take time. Think of it as three months if you want to fully heal." Had I focused solely on "getting over it" by a specific date, I would have missed out on the deeply personal insights that arose during my healing process. Instead of merely recovering physically, I allowed myself to process the emotional aspects of my journey in an open-ended way. This mindset shift unexpectedly led to deeper conversations with others who shared their own stories, providing me with a gift beyond physical restoration. Through this experience, I came to understand the nonlinear nature of healing, which ultimately propelled me toward greater transformation.

This approach to releasing attachment to outcomes aligns with the concept of psychological flexibility—the ability to adapt one's thoughts and behaviors in response to changing circumstances. Research by Kashdan and Rottenberg[10] highlights that psychological flexibility is a key factor in reducing PTSD symptoms and enhancing overall well-being. By relinquishing rigid expectations, we can navigate life's uncertainties with greater confidence and adaptability.

Freeing yourself from strict outcomes also allows you to enjoy the process and the journey, which should be part of your healing, not a trigger to your fears. It also allows you to evolve and venture into new spaces and experiences with a different resolve. Rather than viewing the journey as a series of obstacles, we can embrace it as an opportunity for growth and self-discovery. This shift in perspective liberates us from the fear of failure or deviation from a predetermined path. When we become less fixated on specific outcomes, we open ourselves to new experiences and opportunities, enabling us to move forward with greater ease and curiosity.

If we translate this to a professional arena, relinquishing a strict set of expectations can also foster our creativity and innovation in problem-solving. Rather than forcing ourselves to conform to a self-imposed expectation and set of outcomes, we can experiment with different modalities and approaches. This openness allows us to discover what truly works, rather than what we assume *should* work. Often, the most valuable breakthroughs emerge from unexpected sources—moments of trial and exploration that lead to outcomes beyond what we originally envisioned.

By cultivating a mindset that embraces fluidity, we position ourselves for sustained growth, both personally and professionally. The ability to adapt, learn, and evolve—rather than rigidly adhering to predefined expectations—empowers us to more successfully navigate challenges and uncover opportunities we might have otherwise overlooked. Ultimately, when we let go of attachment to outcomes, we create space for transformation, discovery, and the kind of progress that is both meaningful and sustainable.

Spirit Animals

> "The tiger is the fighter in me. She shows up at times that I need her the most, but I need to be paying attention to see her."
>
> **—Khirma Eliazov, founder of Kika**

The concept of spirit animals is more than just folklore; it aligns with established psychological frameworks that explain how humans process emotions, form identities, and cope with stress. In the traditions of various Indigenous groups, it represents a guiding force, a protector, or the embodiment of personal traits. In more modern discussions, the concept has evolved into a metaphor for self-exploration, metaphysical beliefs, and even popular culture.

Spirit animals have long been associated with personal identity and self-discovery. From a psychological standpoint, they connect to themes of archetypes, subconscious projection, and symbolic interactionism. Studies suggest that spirit animals act as psychological tools, aiding individuals in navigating emotions, finding personal meaning, and coping with trauma. Carl Jung's theory of the collective unconscious proposes that humans share inherited symbolic patterns—archetypes—that shape thoughts, emotions, and behaviors. Animals frequently appear in myths and dreams, representing these universal themes. Other research highlights the interplay between psychology and spirituality, illustrating how animal symbolism bridges personal identity and the subconscious mind.

For Khirma Eliazov, co-founder of Residency Studios and founder of Kika, her spirit animal has been a guiding force throughout her life's transitions. Now in her later 40s, married and with a daughter, Khirma reflects on a life once driven by adrenaline—a pattern that ultimately took a toll on her well-being.

Khirma's career started at age 22 in merchandising at Tommy Hilfiger, and then she moved into positions within Conde Nast at high-profile publications such as *Harper's Bazaar*, *Elle*, and *Vogue*, and eventually founded her own events company called Freestyle. Through her experience in merchandising, in events, and with her editorial prowess, in her late 20s she launched her own handbag line, which was covered in every notable fashion publication and sold globally everywhere from Bergdorf to Saks and beyond. However, although she was thriving through her fast-paced professional growth, she began suffering from fainting spells and fatigue due to working without creating space for her personal well-being. At that time well-being wasn't even on her radar. Khirma simply continued to just power through to achieve her professional success.

At 40, she found a new kind of success. She found the person she wanted to build a family with. She felt grounded in love, and she knew he was her person. In their journey she endured a devastating miscarriage that required a D&C procedure. While healing through their loss, they were still committed to growing their family. What she didn't realize until trying to have a baby again was that while she had relied on adrenaline so much in other parts of her life, her body was giving up. She underwent multiple egg retrievals before turning to

Dr. Gabrielle Francis, a naturopathic doctor. In her analysis, Dr. Francis discovered that Khirma's body was severely deficient in nutrients and minerals, impairing her ability to conceive again. Through investing in a detoxifying and adrenal-rebuilding regimen, she restored her body's balance and resilience.

As she refocused to care for herself in a way she had neglected, Khirma embraced more holistic healing methods in combination with Western medicine, and along the way it deepened her connection to her spirit animal—the tiger. While she had always resonated with its symbolism, meditation and introspection unveiled a deeper awakening to her spiritual bond.

In looking at the symbolism of the spirt animals, the tiger is known to embody strength, courage, and raw instinct. Across cultures and traditions, it is seen as a powerful feline and revered as a symbol of independence, confidence, and resilience. According to the *Dictionary of Symbolism*,[11] the tiger teaches the importance of embracing one's primal instincts while maintaining balance and control. It encourages those who identify with its energy to trust their intuition, take decisive action, and walk their path with unwavering confidence. In dream interpretation, the presence of a tiger may signal a need to harness inner strength, confront fears, or assert dominance in a particular aspect of life.

Khirma's connection to the tiger has served her when she feels stuck or finds herself shutting down and trapped emotionally by all she had gone through over the past several decades. She recognizes how past habits—though once beneficial—became limiting cycles, preventing her from fully healing. Before conceiving in the midst of her IVF journey, during a meditative session, she visualized a tiger alongside a baby, a vision she interpreted as her future self. Subsequent meditative experiences reinforced this connection, as she felt a sense of release and healing.

Today Khirma holds a deeper connection to her spirit animal, and channels it in moments of emotional triggers and a guide for self-reflection when she needs it. She calls these her "eye of the tiger" moments. It's an eye that gives her clarity when emotional triggers kick in and sends her reminders of the importance of investing time in herself, including activities like meditation, working out, and spending time with friends. This shift in focus brought her happiness and a renewed sense of purpose. It's also been the inspiration for the name of her new company, Kika, whose mission is to make it easy and fun to put wellness first for families.

The concept of spirit animals, rooted in both Indigenous traditions and modern psychology, offers another possible lens for self-exploration. Whether through Jungian archetypes, cognitive symbolism, or trauma recovery, the belief in spirit animals serves as a meaningful psychological mechanism for many individuals. For Khirma, the tiger embodies her inner strength and resilience, guiding her through personal and professional transformations. Her journey from an adrenaline-fueled lifestyle to one centered on holistic healing illustrates the potential impact one can experience from spirit animal symbolism. By reconnecting with herself through meditation and wellness practices, she has found clarity, balance, and a renewed sense of purpose and personal growth.

Creating Your Tool Kit

As explored in this chapter, healing from PTSD is not about reaching a fixed destination—it's a continuous journey of learning, growing, and embracing life's complexities. A crucial part of this process is discovering the tools and support systems that resonate with you personally. These tools help you navigate moments and situations that may feel like triggering setbacks, allowing you to regain control. Whether it's shifting your mindset to find silver linings, letting go of rigid expectations, or exploring self-discovery through personal symbolism, the most important step is identifying what best supports your growth.

Building on the action steps outlined earlier in this chapter to break cycles of negative thinking and reduce anxiety, the following strategies will help you develop or enhance your personal toolkit. While many of these methods have been introduced in previous sections, here we highlight real-life examples of how women have successfully integrated them into their healing journeys.

Strategies that Align from Stories Shared

- **Mindfulness and meditation:** Staying present without judgment reduces negative thought patterns and enhances emotional regulation.
  - Khirma prioritizes her mindfulness practice by protecting the time she sets aside for it. Every morning, she dedicates 15 minutes to quiet reflection, allowing her to release emotional weight and set a clear intention for the day ahead.
- **Journaling and thought recording:** Writing down thoughts helps identify patterns and triggers, externalizing anxieties and making them easier to challenge.
  - Shirley (introduced in Chapter 1) used journaling as a tool for self-discovery. This practice led to revelations about her stroke, ultimately inspiring her to write her book, *Thoughts of a Butterfly*.
- **Physical movement and deep breathing:** Engaging in yoga, exercise, or breathwork lowers cortisol levels, promotes relaxation, and rewires the mindset.
  - Antonia, an experienced yoga practitioner, relies on Kundalini yoga—a powerful practice combining breathwork, movement, chanting, and meditation. She emphasizes the importance of choosing a practice suited to your personal journey and emotional readiness, as some methods can trigger strong emotional releases.
- **Social support and therapy:** As explored in Chapter 6, seeking support allows you to process emotions, gain perspective, and release the burden of facing anxiety alone.
  - Among women, there is a recognition that that community support evolves with personal growth. The key is to find a support system that aligns with your changing needs and desires over time.

(*continued*)

(*continued*)

- **Positive affirmations and self-compassion:** Replacing self-criticism with affirming, encouraging self-talk reduces anxiety-driven self-doubt.
  - Lisa Mateo uses a simple yet powerful method (one that I share as a practice, too): leaving sticky notes with positive affirmations for herself and her daughter, reinforcing a daily practice of self-compassion.

Expanding Our Toolkit: New Strategies to Explore

- **Behavioral actions:** Gradually testing small actions helps disprove irrational fears, reducing avoidance behaviors and building confidence.
  - *Example:* If you fear singing in front of others, start by humming in a small group, progress to singing softly to a friend, and eventually perform a full song before an audience. Observing your fear lessen with each step reinforces personal growth. In 2024, I decided to experiment with this by taking singing lessons. Each month, I have slowly come out of my shell and that freedom has translated in so many ways!
- **Exposure therapy:** Facing fears gradually, rather than avoiding them, weakens the fear response over time.
  - *Example:* If public speaking causes anxiety, begin by asking questions in familiar settings. Progress to speaking in small internal meetings, then participate in a panel discussion with preplanned questions before working up to a keynote presentation.
- **And let's not forget the power of sleep!** Implementing healthy sleep habits and relaxation techniques supports a well-rested brain which can better process stress better and reduces anxiety triggers.

The journey of healing is deeply personal, and so is the toolkit we build and employ throughout the process. The key is to be open to experimenting with different strategies, remain open to growth, and refine what works best for you along the way. Healing isn't linear—it's about progress, not perfection, as is our growth. By equipping ourselves with the right tools, we can navigate challenges with greater confidence, inner strength and self-compassion. So stay explorative, keep evolving, and trust in your ability to create a path toward healing that truly supports you.

Chapter 8 Contributors:

Dr. Meg Hainer, Trish Barillas, Khirma Eliazov, Tai Beauchamp, Antonia Saint Dunbar, Kristy Lynn, Joelle Oliver, Jill Katz.

9

The Dance Between Growth and Shedding

Navigating Positive Transformation and Letting Go of What No Longer Serves You

When I stepped away from my career on Wall Street, I embarked on a commitment to take a six-month journey of self-discovery. One of first stops on this path was joining the LABrynth Theater Company, a space where creativity, emotion, and self-exploration intertwined. Immersing myself in acting and theater was one of my ways of saying "yes" to an EVOLVING time in my life, embracing the unknown, and opening myself to lessons beyond my professional expertise. It was here that I uncovered truths about myself in ways I had never anticipated.

At LABrynth, we didn't just perform plays; we engaged in immersive workshops designed to deepen our emotional intelligence and help us connect with our inner selves. One immensely transformative exercise will always stand out in my memory. We were asked to stand up and spontaneously answer this question: "What was the moment that broke you?" and then, without pause, burst into singing the song "Joy and Pain" by Rob Base & DJ E-Z Rock.

I remember thinking, I've got this. I know my answer. Without hesitation, I decided my response would be about an ex who had betrayed me. It seemed like the obvious choice—heartbreak is often assumed to be one of the most painful experiences one can endure. But when I stood up, something unexpected happened. As I opened my mouth, the words that emerged were not the ones I had planned.

"The day my dad left," I articulated.

I stood stunned. The revelation struck me so deeply that I could feel my entire being shaken with the reality of it. In that moment, I broke. And yet, paradoxically, I healed. The words had surfaced from a place buried so deep that even I had been unaware of them and what it had shaped in how I associated breakups with men. And then, as instructed, I began to sing out loud, tears running down my face, "Joy and pain, sunshine and rain . . ."

My father and I have always shared a loving relationship. As an adult, I came to understand that relationships sometimes don't work out and that people must take different paths in search of their own truths and happiness. For him that meant moving to a different part of the country. But in that moment at LABrynth, I realized how much unconscious pain I was carrying. It had subtly influenced my choices, causing me to hold on to unhealthy relationships longer than I should have, as though proving to myself that love doesn't always leave. This single exercise illuminated something I hadn't even known I needed to shed.

Growth often comes from unexpected places. Sometimes it emerges not from relentless striving but from surrender—from allowing ourselves to be vulnerable enough to acknowledge what no longer serves us. In that moment of honesty, I was empowered to release a pain I had unknowingly held onto for years. I was able to tell myself: *This bad relationship is not the same as my father leaving. My dad's love for me never wavered; it evolved, and staying in unhealthy relationships doesn't replace my relationship with him as a little girl.*

We often think of growth as an upward trajectory, a pursuit of more—more success, more achievements, more accolades. But true growth is just as much about letting go as it is about pushing forward. It requires us to shed outdated beliefs, unhealed wounds, and attachments that keep us tethered to past versions of ourselves.

For women in leadership roles or those on the path to leadership, this lesson is particularly crucial. We are often conditioned to equate growth with resilience, determination, and ambition. And while these qualities are invaluable, we must also recognize that growth sometimes means relinquishing things that don't serve us, stepping back to reflect, and allowing space for transformation.

The Inner Work: Shedding for Growth

Doing "the work" isn't just about pushing ourselves to the limit. It's about introspection, reflection, and sometimes painful honesty. It means asking ourselves the hard questions:

- What is holding me back?
- Why is it holding me back?
- What do I need to release?
- What am I afraid to confront?
- Why am I afraid to confront it?

Shedding isn't just about external commitments; it's also about evaluating our internal beliefs and letting go of those beliefs that no longer align with *who we are becoming*. It requires a willingness to be vulnerable—to break open in order to heal, similar to my experience in the exercise at LABrynth. And when we give ourselves permission to be vulnerable, we also give permission to others to do the same. This shared vulnerability fosters collective strength, allows us to lean into our community as we explored in Chapter 6, and create a space where true connection and support can thrive.

Integrating the Journey

Up until this point, we have explored various facets of personal growth and transformation:

- We have examined the law of manifestation and the power of trusting our intuition.

- We have learned about the physiological and emotional impact of stress—both positive and negative.
- We have challenged conventional definitions of external beauty and redefined purpose and priorities.
- We have accepted that in the realm of inner work, there is no perfection—only progress.
- We have embraced the importance of community and sisterhood as pillars of support.
- We have relieved ourselves of the pressure of FOMO and learned to seek more meaningful moments of awe.
- We have armed ourselves with tools to disarm anxiety and cultivate resilience.

Now we bring it all together by exploring how decluttering and shedding—both physically and emotionally—can become a catalyst for growth.

Breaking Down Decluttering and Shedding as Pathways to Expansion

Decluttering is often perceived as a simple act of tidying up physical spaces, but its impact extends far beyond organization. A cluttered room can feel just as burdensome as the emotional and mental clutter we accumulate—old wounds, limiting beliefs, and self-doubt can inhibit personal growth just as much as physical mess does. By addressing clutter in all its forms, we create space not only in our environment but also in our minds, leading to enhanced well-being and self-expansion.

The benefits of decluttering extend well beyond aesthetics or physical order. Making space in our lives—whether by cleaning out a closet, clearing a busy schedule, or letting go of outdated mindsets—can lead to increased confidence, heightened self-efficacy, and improved mental clarity. When we engage in decluttering, we actively make choices about what serves us and what does not. This decision-making process strengthens our problem-solving abilities and fosters a sense of agency over our lives. Furthermore, organizing and simplifying our surroundings can be energizing, shifting us into a productive mindset that fuels motivation and confidence.

Decluttering applies to many aspects of life beyond physical spaces. It can involve reassessing commitments, relationships, and even digital spaces. For example, an overloaded calendar can lead to burnout, leaving little room for creativity, rest, or meaningful connections. By decluttering our schedules, setting boundaries, and learning to say no to obligations that do not align with our values or priorities, we create a more balanced and fulfilling life. Similarly, digital clutter—such as an overflowing inbox or excessive social media consumption—can be overwhelming. Organizing our digital space and setting intentional limits on screen time can lead to greater focus and mental clarity.

Beyond its practical benefits, decluttering serves as a powerful tool for self-reflection and emotional regulation. As we sort through our possessions, our commitments, and our thoughts, we gain insight into our habits, attachments, and emotional triggers. This heightened self-awareness enables us to align our actions with our true values and aspirations. Additionally, decluttering creates the mental space necessary for a wandering mind—a state that is often associated with creativity, problem-solving, and innovative thinking. Research suggests that allowing our minds to roam freely can lead to creative insights and cognitive rejuvenation, especially after periods of intense focus.[1]

Mental clutter, much like physical mess, can also be overwhelming. Worries, distractions, and excessive information intake can cloud our judgment and make decision-making more difficult. Emotional decluttering, which involves releasing toxic thoughts or relationships that don't serve us is essential for fostering a positive mindset. This process requires recognizing and letting go of relationships and commitments that drain our energy or hinder personal growth. Practices such as therapy, meditation, and journaling can support emotional decluttering, helping us process emotions and cultivate a healthier, more intentional mindset.

Shedding, as a deeper extension of decluttering, involves not just removing what is unnecessary but fundamentally transforming ourselves by letting go of outdated beliefs, identities, and attachments. Shedding requires introspection and courage, because it often involves releasing aspects of ourselves that have provided comfort or security but no longer serve our highest potential or our greater purpose.

For example, shedding *the need* for acceptance is as liberating as decluttering a cluttered workspace. Persistently chasing acceptance often stems from fear—fear of failure, judgment, or inadequacy. However, by releasing this burden, we open ourselves to greater creativity, flexibility, and self-compassion because we relieve ourselves from worrying about outside ridicule. Similarly, shedding self-imposed limitations—whether they are doubts about our abilities or us harboring societal expectations—allows us to step into new opportunities and evolve into our fullest selves.

Shedding is closely tied to the success of our ongoing personal transformation, because as we grow, we outgrow certain identities, relationships, and belief systems. Holding onto these outdated aspects can create resistance to change and hinder our self-expansion. The process of shedding invites us to embrace uncertainty and trust that by releasing what no longer aligns with our true selves, we make space for new growth, deeper connections, and a more authentic way of living.

Ultimately, decluttering and shedding are interconnected pathways to expansion. Decluttering helps clear the external and mental space necessary for clarity and focus, while shedding allows for profound internal transformation. By consciously engaging in both processes, we cultivate a path that is not only organized but also more aligned with our highest aspirations. Through this journey of letting go, we gain not just a cleaner space but a renewed sense of purpose, new freedoms, and a personal evolution.

A Visualization Illustrating the Relationship of Decluttering and Shedding

Facet	Decluttering	Shedding
Our Focus	Material and surface-level changes	Emotional and spiritual shifts
Our Process	Systematic and structured	Introspective
Outcomes	Increased self-awareness	Enhanced self-evolution and authenticity

The Empowerment of Decluttering and Making Space for the Energy That Fuels You

Building upon our journey of identifying what fuels positive stress versus negative stress, diving into purpose, and reprioritizing our lives, let's explore the deep opportunity that decluttering presents.

Decluttering manifests in many forms. It may involve removing unused objects—such as clothes gathering dust in the closet—or distancing ourselves from relationships that no longer align with our well-being. At its core, decluttering allows us to create a more intentional, structured environment that fosters clarity, productivity, and peace of mind.

Let's meet Yvette Vargas, an esteemed professional and current executive vice president of development at Citizens Bank. With over a decade at the bank, she is responsible for defining and leading development strategies related to talent management, leadership, and organizational development. Throughout her multi-decade career, Yvette has developed a well-established playbook for organizational strategies and optimization.

In 2024, recognizing a gap between how she approached organization in her professional life versus her personal life, Yvette decided to take a fresh approach to her New Year's resolutions. Rather than setting a traditional resolution, she chose a guiding principle to steer her decisions and keep herself accountable to her vision. She named it "The Year of Decluttering." A woman with a deep appreciation for fashion, Yvette possesses a wardrobe that many would envy. From head to toe, she is impeccably dressed, and she can name every designer in her closet without hesitation.

However, as she entered a new life chapter and navigated personal health challenges, she realized that her overflowing wardrobe no longer aligned with her evolving self. Determined to declutter, she meticulously evaluated each piece, keeping only what truly brought her joy and confidence. This process became more than an organizational task—it evolved into a metaphor for self-exploration and transformation for the year.

This journey prompted her to reflect deeply on fundamental questions: "What is the meaning of life?" "Are we truly living the life we want?" "How accountable are we for the choices we make?" These inquiries also reinforced the notion that decluttering is not merely a solo endeavor. Yvette came to understand that achieving meaningful decluttering required external support. She sought out a community of like-minded individuals who could help her stay disciplined and committed to her journey. As we explored in Chapter 6, growth is often most effective when shared, and Yvette's experience further confirmed this idea. And each time, Yvette felt she was hitting a setback in her process, she had both her community and herself to lean on to learn from those pauses and get through the moments to her next milestone of victory.

While decluttering physical possessions may be straightforward, the true challenge lies in letting go of the emotional baggage that may exist with those physical objects. Through self-reflection, we can gain clarity about who we truly are and why that impacts what we hold onto. As discussed in Chapter 4, everyone has unique tendencies and needs, making the decluttering process deeply personal. The key is to intentionally evaluate what enhances our lives and what does not.

In our journey of self-reflection, we deepen our self-awareness, awareness of our individual personalities, tendencies, and needs, and that shapes how we approach decluttering. This means that decluttering will look different for everyone. Some may find fulfillment in minimalism, while others may thrive in a space filled with meaningful objects. The essential principle is to intentionally assess whether the things we keep add value to our lives or create stress and stagnation.

When we intentionally declutter, we free up mental and emotional energy that can be redirected toward our passions, relationships, and aspirations. And we can realize that: decluttering is not about deprivation—it's about making room for what truly matters. It is a continuous process of refinement and alignment, ensuring that our surroundings and inner world reflect our truest desires and purpose. Whether through removing unnecessary material possessions, letting go of outdated beliefs, or reevaluating commitments, decluttering allows us to step into a more fulfilling and purpose-driven existence.

As a first exercise in this chapter, let's work on a few key steps to successfully embark on the practice of decluttering:

- **Define your goals.** Determine why you want to declutter and how it supports your broader vision. Is it to create a more organized space? Simplify your life? Foster mental clarity?
- **Start small.** Focus on manageable tasks to build momentum. For example, if decluttering your wardrobe feels overwhelming, begin with a single drawer or shelf.
- **Schedule regular sessions.** Commit to a schedule—whether weekly or monthly—and set milestones to track progress.
- **Check in with your true self.** Create intentional habits to prevent future clutter. Establish a "gut check" phrase to reinforce mindful decision-making when tempted to accumulate more.

By consciously removing clutter, we create room for the energy, people, and opportunities that truly fuel us. The process empowers us to move forward with greater clarity, purpose, and authenticity.

Letting Go of Relationships That No Longer Serve Personal Growth

> "If you have friends who covet what you have, you can never fully trust intentions, and that becomes a hinderance on you."
>
> —**Anonymous**

Building upon the decluttering of objects, growth often also means releasing relationships, commitments, and self-imposed pressures that no longer serve us as well. Letting go of good relationships that hinder personal growth is one of the most challenging yet necessary steps on the path to self-discovery and emotional well-being. Whether it is a friendship that has turned toxic, a romantic partnership that no longer aligns with our values, or a professional connection that has outlived its purpose, recognizing when and how to release these ties is essential for maintaining inner peace and fulfillment.

Unlike decluttering material possessions, parting with relationships can be more complex. The emotional bonds we form with people are deeply interwoven with our experiences, memories, and sense of identity. However, holding onto relationships that no longer serve our highest good can tether us to negative emotions, unhealthy competition, and lingering resentment. Over time, these dynamics can weigh heavily on our mental and emotional health, leaving us feeling drained rather than uplifted.

As explored in Chapter 6, not all relationships are meant to last a lifetime. Some individuals enter our lives to teach valuable lessons, offer companionship for a particular season, or reflect who we are at a given moment. As we evolve, our needs, values, and capacity to give and receive love also change. This natural progression often requires us to reevaluate our connections and make difficult decisions about who should remain in our inner circle.

> "Givers have to set limits, because takers never do."
>
> **—Anonymous**

Some relationships nourish our souls and encourage us to become our best selves. They energize us, bring out our strengths, and add to our well-being. These connections act as catalysts for growth, offering support, joy, and positivity. Others, however, may drain us, introducing toxicity, excessive demands, and a lack of reciprocity. These relationships deplete our emotional resources, making it difficult to focus on our aspirations and overall well-being.

The process of disengaging from unhelpful relationships is not just about cutting ties—it's about reclaiming your energy, setting boundaries, and prioritizing your personal growth. The first step in letting go is developing awareness of the signs that a relationship is no longer serving you. Often, we stay in unfulfilling relationships out of habit, guilt, or fear of change. However, recognizing certain signals allows us to make informed decisions about which relationships to nurture and which to release.

Signs that a relationship may no longer serve you:

- **Emotional exhaustion:** Do you feel drained after interactions rather than uplifted?
- **Lack of mutual support:** Are you consistently giving without receiving in return?
- **Manipulation and control:** Do you often feel coerced, guilted, or pressured into actions that don't align with your values?
- **Stagnation:** Is there a lack of growth or personal development within the relationship?
- **Compromised identity:** Are you feeling unable to be your authentic self as a result of fear of judgment or rejection?

As you take stock, you realize these dynamics can emerge in any sphere—friendships, family relationships, romantic partnerships, or professional settings. If a relationship consistently leaves you feeling diminished, it may be time to step back and reassess its place in your life.

Once you recognize that a relationship is no longer beneficial, there are strategies you can embrace for letting go and/or for setting boundaries. Taking the deliberate steps to distance yourself can feel both liberating and uncomfortable. However, by identifying patterns and seeing them for what they are, you can begin to say, "No, this is not for me," with greater confidence and less guilt. Some people will be energy givers, while others will be energy vampires. For your personal growth, happiness, and evolution, it is essential to limit your time with energy vampires and reduce emotional investment in one-sided relationships.

Letting go is a process but by prioritizing self-care and practicing mindfulness, as explored in earlier chapters, we gain powerful tools in navigating these transitions. Because, even when we intellectually understand that a relationship is no longer good for us, our emotions may resist change. By staying present, also explored throughout this book, we can prevent ourselves from ruminating and second-guessing our needs. Instead, we learn to honor our emotions without judgment and detach with compassion, free from resentment or guilt.

Establishing boundaries is another essential step when distancing yourself from an unhealthy relationship. This might involve limiting interactions, politely declining invitations, or having an honest conversation about your need for space. Initially, guilt may arise when walking away from a relationship, stemming from a fear of abandoning someone or being perceived as selfish. However, reframing the situation as an act of self-growth rather than failure can ease this emotional burden. Every relationship serves a purpose, and recognizing when its chapter has ended is a sign of emotional intelligence.

As a second exercise in this chapter, here are practical strategies you can take for letting go:

- **Identify patterns** (*picking from signs listed on the prior page*). Ask yourself if the relationship is consistently draining, stagnant, or requiring perpetual compromise.
- **Set boundaries.** Limit interactions, politely decline invitations, or have an honest conversation about your need for space.
- **Reframe your mindset.** View letting go as an act of self-growth rather than a failure. Recognizing when a relationship has served its purpose is a sign of maturity.
- **Prioritize self-care.** Even when you intellectually recognize an unhealthy relationship, emotions may resist change. Cultivate inner peace and presence through mindfulness to embrace what is, rather than dwell on what was.
- **Express gratitude.** Rather than harboring resentment or pain, acknowledge the relationship for the experiences and lessons it provided. Every connection teaches us something. Express gratitude for the positive moments, allowing for closure and emotional peace.

Decluttering and letting go of relationships that no longer serve personal growth is not an easy process, but it is essential for mental well-being. It is crucial to remember that decluttering relationships is not about discarding people thoughtlessly—it is about honoring your personal evolution. Every relationship teaches us something, and recognizing when it is time to move on is an act of self-respect. By acknowledging unhealthy patterns, setting boundaries, practicing mindfulness, and seeking support, we create space for new opportunities, deeper connections, and a more authentic version of ourselves as we grow and evolve.

Shedding the Past to Thrive in Your Future—Doing the Work on Losing Inhibitions

Beyond objects and people, shedding self-imposed limitations is a deeply internal exploration. Often, subconscious beliefs and unresolved traumas limit our potential. Even when we believe we are intellectually aware, emotional awareness can still be elusive. This disconnect can prevent us from recognizing the outdated beliefs that shape our actions, relationships, and perceptions of ourselves.

Reflecting on my story shared earlier in this chapter, I realized that while I was intellectually aware of feeling sad as a little girl when my dad left for the military, I was emotionally unaware of how that experience shaped my ability to let go of romantic relationships that no longer served me. Unconsciously, I held onto an outdated belief that rejection was a reflection of my shortcomings, causing me to chase acceptance out of fear of failure or inadequacy. However, by recognizing and releasing this false belief, I was able to make better decisions, leave toxic relationships with conviction, and ultimately, it led me to meet my now-husband.

Traumatic experiences, especially those encountered in childhood, can significantly shape our self-perception and worldview. According to research published in the *Journal of Traumatic Stress*, unprocessed childhood traumas can lead to negative belief systems and emotional dysregulation in adulthood.[2] These subconscious beliefs can manifest as fear of rejection, feelings of inadequacy, or imposter syndrome, ultimately limiting our growth and fulfillment.

Outdated beliefs can stem from early experiences, cultural expectations, or societal pressures. For example, a child who feels abandoned may develop a belief that they are unlovable or not good enough. These beliefs become ingrained, influencing their adult relationships and self-worth. Shedding these outdated narratives involves identifying their origins, questioning their validity, and consciously choosing new, empowering beliefs.

Shedding requires courageous introspection. It involves examining our emotional responses and challenging the beliefs that no longer serve us. When we embrace this process, we gain the power to break free from self-imposed limitations, opening ourselves to new possibilities.

During my interviews, I listened to numerous examples of women unconsciously held back by past experiences that shaped tightly held beliefs. These beliefs impacted their growth in various areas, from public speaking fears to relationship building, to feeling unworthy of their successes.

One deeply profound example comes from a prominent woman who has held leadership roles across Fortune 500 and large private companies. Despite her accomplishments and leadership, she found herself experiencing a sudden onset of anxiety and near panic attacks during public speaking.

Surprised by the intensity of her symptoms and realizing that avoidance of public speaking was a barrier, she knew she had to better understand the root cause. With the support of her doctor and her long-standing therapist, she realized that her symptoms were linked to the onset of early menopause and were exacerbated by a familial history of anxiety and depression. Her maternal grandmother had likely experienced similar hormonal swings, and had committed suicide by asphyxiation in her 50s.This trauma unconsciously shaped her relationship with breath and contributed to her anxiety about public speaking.

According to the American Psychological Association, intergenerational trauma can impact emotional regulation and stress responses in subsequent generations.[3] In her case, this trauma influenced her ability to manage anxiety and caused her to associate breathwork with fear rather than calm. Confronting this trauma was painful but liberating. It took exploration, openness, and deep compassion. By accepting the painful family burden, and managing her physical symptoms with hormone replacement therapy (HRT), she reframed her relationship with breath, allowing her to find peace and confidence in public speaking.

Her story demonstrates the power of shedding to overcome deeply rooted fears. It also highlights the importance of understanding the origins of our anxieties to heal and grow. As she continued to release the outdated beliefs tied to her trauma, she has found new confidence. Today, she speaks on podcasts, guest lectures, and conferences globally.

Shedding self-imposed limitations requires introspection, vulnerability, and the courage to confront painful experiences. By releasing outdated beliefs and traumas, we open ourselves to growth and new possibilities. Her journey shows how shedding can transform fear into empowerment, reminding us that personal growth involves confronting hidden barriers and doing the necessary inner work to thrive in the future.

Shedding is a process. As a third exercise, here are a few key steps to successfully embark on the practice of shedding outdated beliefs:

- **Practice mindfulness and self-awareness.** Tap into what we have explored in this book. Allow yourself to be aware of your thoughts, emotions, and reactions. Observe the beliefs you hold without judgment and allow yourself to identify patterns.
- **Reflect and identify root causes.** This is a journaling opportunity. When you observe a moment, write it down. What did you feel, what are your fears coming from, what do you think is limiting you?
- **Challenge your beliefs.** As you identify root causes, challenge their validity. This is where your cognitive work can come in. Is it something you need to work through, or can you replace your negative beliefs with empowering positive affirmations and a new perspective?
- **Tap your support network.** As exemplified through many stories, there is power in your community and/or in one-on-one therapy. If the root cause is deeply rooted or

(*continued*)

(*continued*)

hard to identify, consider allowing others in to help you on your journey. From EMDR, as channeled by Lisa in Chapter 6, or communities, like the one started by Trish, be open to consider what works for you.

- **Practice self-compassion.** Cultivate self-compassion along your journey. Embrace that it will have progress and setbacks and both are forms of growth. Treat yourself with the kindness you would a best friend and release yourself from self-blame.
- **Create new experiences along the way.** Along your journey, rewire how you respond to things, as explored in Chapter 7 with Chiara and Jennifer and moments of awe. Challenge old beliefs by creating new positive narratives.

Over time, by practicing these strategies consistently, you can gradually let go of outdated beliefs and traumas, opening yourself to personal growth and fulfillment.

Growth and Shedding as a Parallel Evolution

The concept of growth and shedding as a parallel evolution in our personal development explores the dynamic interplay between personal growth and the simultaneous release of outdated beliefs, habits, or self-inflicted identities. This dual process mirrors the natural cycles of evolution we observe in the environment we live in, suggesting that personal development involves both the cultivation of new qualities and the shedding of those that no longer serve us.

Decluttering is the first step toward the process of shedding, focused on objects, belongings, schedules, people … and it contributes to our evolution as we grow. With shedding we go even deeper.

Personal growth is often viewed as a goal-oriented endeavor, focusing on acquiring new skills, new knowledge, and adopting new behaviors. However, there is a distinguishing difference between personal growth and personal evolution. Personal growth implies changing aspects of oneself, whereas personal evolution involves radically accepting who you are and allowing larger changes to occur. This perspective emphasizes the importance of self-acceptance and the unfolding of one's greatest self.

Personal evolution requires analyzing information and contemplating the person you aspire to become, with your purpose at the core of this analysis. It involves a conscious effort to align our actions with our core values and authentic self, leading to a more integrated and harmonious existence.

Integral to personal development is the process of shedding—releasing outdated beliefs, habits, or identities that hinder growth. This concept aligns with the idea of positive disintegration, a theory proposed by Kazimierz Dąbrowski. Through his firsthand experience with the tragic outcomes of war, Dąbrowski observed that some individuals fell apart, while others experienced meaningful personal growth. As many others did before him, and many have done since, he asked, "Why?" The answer he put together to this question became the theory of positive disintegration, which in turn laid the foundation for modern theories of post-traumatic growth.

Positive disintegration suggests that personal growth often involves a period of inner conflict and disintegration of those beliefs that don't serve you, leading to the emergence of a more authentic self. This process requires individuals to confront and release aspects of themselves that no longer align with their evolving values and goals.[4]

Like decluttering, the act of shedding is not about discarding; it is a transformative process that allows us to make room for new growth. By letting go of limiting beliefs and behaviors, we can embrace new possibilities and directions in our personal development journey.

The concept of parallel evolution in personal development suggests that growth and shedding often occur simultaneously, each influencing and enhancing the other. As we grow and develop new skills and perspectives, we may also recognize and release aspects of ourselves that no longer serve our evolving identity. This dual process leads to a more holistic and integrated sense of self.

Theories suggest that we progress along multiple quasi-independent lines of personal growth, which are parallel and occur simultaneously, albeit at different rates. For example, one may experience personal growth in emotional intelligence while simultaneously shedding outdated self-esteem issues. This parallel progression allows for a more comprehensive and balanced development.[5]

If we think back to Chapter 4 and Maslow's hierarchy of needs, there is a pyramid of multiple elements that factor into why we pursue one need over others. We have physiological needs, safety and security, love and belonging, self-esteem, and self-actualization (as the most advanced). Weaving that with lessons we explored throughout this book, we can see within those needs there are stages into our personal growth such as recognition, learning, expressing, awareness, acceptance, and letting go, awakening to your purpose and evolution.

Understanding the interplay between growth and shedding can have practical implications for personal development. Recognizing that personal evolution involves both the cultivation of new qualities and the release of outdated ones can lead to a more balanced and authentic life. This awareness can help us navigate the challenges of personal development with greater resilience and self-compassion.

Shedding by Leaning into Your Purpose to Fuel Professional Growth

> "I was once asked: If I were to write my obituary, what would I want it to say? My response: legacy, impact, and inspiration."
>
> **—Modupé Whyelaé Rouse, founder, Finally Free Brands**

If you met Modupé Whyelaé Rouse, you would be struck by her presence—a radiant energy that emanates from within. She greets you with a warm smile, embodying a spirit of purpose and a deep commitment to fostering universal access and equity. Her professional journey has been impressive, with leadership roles at major global corporations, including Amazon and Cisco Systems. She has served as the global director of inclusive experience and technology for Amazon Stores and sits on the boards of esteemed organizations, including the National Black MBA Association and digitalundivided.

But beyond her professional accomplishments, Modupé is a woman who exemplifies the transformative power of shedding—letting go of limitations, pain, and outdated beliefs to embrace growth and evolution.

She possesses an extraordinary level of self-awareness, emotional intelligence, and the ability to reframe adversity into resilience. Her journey is a testament to how one can rise from deep challenges, not just surviving but thriving, with renewed purpose and clarity.

Modupe's life has been marked by trials that many would find insurmountable. As a child, she experienced sexual abuse so early in life that it took until adulthood for her subconscious to reveal the truth. For a long time, the fragmented memories manifested as frozen moments of visual flashbacks—until she had the ability to acknowledge and process them as an adult.

The loss of her 18-month-old son was a devastation so deep that it left an indelible wound on her heart. And then years later, the pain was reopened when her best friend's son, also her godson, passed away from cancer at the age of 16. She and her daughters were by his side during his final moments, reliving the echoes of grief they had fought so hard to heal from.

These heartbreaks, compounded by a painful divorce and holding leadership positions in arenas where she was often a sole voice aiming to bring equity and inclusion to the corporate workplace at a time when roles of this focus were being eliminated on a large scale, all led to an ongoing inner battle not to feel like a failure, defeated, or depressed.

"God, I just want to be in love with myself."

—Prayer request put out by Modupé

This seemingly simple but clear request for help prayer became a catalyst for her healing. She knew that if she wanted to move forward, she had to first shed the emotional burdens that were keeping her down. She needed to redefine success and embrace the fullness of her journey—not just the triumphs, but also the pain, growth, and evolution that came with it.

Through therapy, deep introspection, and a move to Atlanta, Modupé began to rebuild herself. Atlanta symbolized a fresh start, a space where she could feel free from the pain of past traumas. She realized that healing is not linear, and that the ability to heal from grief can resurface in unexpected ways. The loss of her godson was not just a personal heartbreak; it was also a powerful moment of healing for her daughters, who had been processing the death of their brother for years. It was through this lens that Modupé began to understand the interconnectedness of loss, healing, and purpose.

Her perspective shifted. Instead of seeing her past as a source of shame, she began to view it as a foundation of strength. She asked herself: *How can I take the curtain of shame that surrounds me and transform it into drapes of glory? How can I look at my battle scars and see them as the marks of a warrior who has not only survived but has emerged wiser, stronger, and filled with love for herself?*

Embracing a New Definition of Success

With growth comes the necessity to shed what no longer serves us. Modupé has shed many beliefs that once constrained her:

- The belief that success must follow a singular, predefined path
- The notion that her success must mirror someone else's to be valid
- The pressure to equate busyness with value and progress

She has embraced the reality that her purpose is not confined to a corporate setting. While she spent much of her career as an executive, she has come to recognize that her true impact extends far beyond titles and boardrooms. She understands that her legacy is one of inspiration, advocacy, and transformation. Whether she is leading within a corporation, building her own venture, mentoring women, or being a mother to her four daughters, her purpose remains the same: to empower others and to create meaningful change.

Today, Modupé stands as a testament to the power of self-love and resilience. Her journey has not been about avoiding pain but rather embracing it as a necessary part of growth. She has learned that true freedom comes from within—it is the release of self-doubt, the acceptance of one's own journey, and the courage to walk in authenticity. Modupé continues to evolve, shedding limiting beliefs, toxic environments, and anything that no longer aligns with her purpose. She understands that healing is not about forgetting the past but about using it as a steppingstone toward a greater purpose.

Modupé's story is an invitation—to those who feel stuck, to those who are battling self-doubt, and to those who are carrying wounds they have yet to heal. Her journey teaches us that growth is a choice we can make. That shedding is necessary. And that purpose, when fully embraced, has the power to fuel both our professional and our personal transformation.

As a final chapter exercise, we will explore effective ways to reflect on two fundamental questions: "What do I want to achieve?" and "How can I get there?"

Each of us has a unique approach that resonates with our personal style. Choosing a method that speaks to you will support your journey of growth and self-improvement. Here are some structured ways to engage in this reflection:

- **Create a vision board.** Assemble a creative collage of images, words, and symbols that represent your ultimate goals and aspirations. While crafting this visual representation of your dreams, it is equally important to identify potential obstacles. Ask yourself, "What is holding me back?" Write these down alongside your goals, and engage in the work of decluttering or shedding any limiting beliefs, habits, or distractions that may hinder your progress.
- **Make a mind map.** This technique involves placing your main goal at the center of a diagram and branching out with related ideas, strategies, and sub-goals. A mind map helps you visually organize your thoughts and identify the necessary steps to reach your objectives. As you examine each target, consider what obstacles might stand in your way. Document these challenges and develop strategies to mitigate or overcome them, ensuring a clearer path toward success.
- **Develop a wheel of life.** This method allows you to assess various aspects of your life—such as well-being, relationships, personal development, and professional growth—by rating your level of satisfaction in each area. Plotting these ratings on a circular diagram provides a visual representation of balance in your life, helping you identify which areas need more attention. This exercise fosters self-reflection and enables you to set specific goals for personal improvement.

As you embark on this journey, remember that the process of decluttering and shedding varies in intensity. Throughout this chapter, we have explored different starting points, from small physical spaces, such as a drawer or desk, to broader aspects of our lives, like time management and relationships. Evaluating how we allocate our time can help us reclaim it in more positive and productive ways. Similarly, reassessing our relationships allows us to determine which connections continue to fuel our growth and which may no longer serve us in our current life stage.

Sometimes the work of personal growth and transformation requires an even deeper examination. We may need to confront ingrained beliefs, whether conscious or subconscious, that hold us back. By recognizing, understanding, accepting, and, when necessary, releasing these limitations, we create space for continued development and self-discovery.

It is important to acknowledge that this journey does not have to be undertaken alone. Seeking support when needed is not a sign of weakness but rather a demonstration of strength and self-awareness. Whether through mentorship, coaching, or community, having a support system can make the process of decluttering, shedding, and growing more effective and fulfilling.

By engaging in these reflective practices and embracing the process of letting go, we empower ourselves to take ownership of our narratives and reclaim our personal agency. Growth is a continuous journey, and by actively participating in it, we set the stage for a more intentional, fulfilling, and purpose-driven life.

Chapter 9 Contributors:

Yvette Vargas, Clarissa Ramos-Cafarelli, Alexis Thomas, Kristy Lynn, Modupé Whyelaé Rouse

Concluding Thoughts and Applying the Work

THROUGHOUT THIS JOURNEY, we have explored the experiences of women—including myself—who have encountered many of the same challenges, questions, and revelations that you, as a reader, may also face. The collective goal of this book has been to demystify the barriers that often hold us back from leading a purpose-driven life, one where we prioritize nurturing our mental and physical well-being our leadership path.

The insights and principles we've explored throughout this book are not merely theoretical—they are meant to be lived. To support you in bringing these lessons into your daily life, the following appendix section contains practical exercises and tools designed to help you integrate these concepts with intention and action.

The self-discovery worksheet serves as the foundation for your personal exploration. Through guided reflection, you will examine key elements such as self-confidence, a growth-oriented mindset, your unique purpose and passions, and the role of relationships in shaping your journey. This exercise will provide clarity on where you stand today and where you aspire to grow.

As we explored in Chapter 4, mindset is a powerful determinant of our trajectory. You will create your own affirmations to reinforce the priorities you aim to set, ensuring that what truly matters finds its place on your "important list." Building on the lessons from Chapter 6, you will deepen your commitment to personal empowerment with the "Mirror, Mirror on the Wall" exercise, where you will craft "I Will" statements that reinforce your evolving self-perception and confidence.

Recognizing the importance of energy management, you will reflect on the activities that energize you versus those that drain you. By identifying tasks that can be delegated, you create space to operate from your highest self, prioritizing what aligns with your purpose while reducing unnecessary stressors. This practice allows you to shift focus toward the positive stressors that challenge and inspire you, rather than the negative stressors that weigh you down.

Understanding that our environments play a critical role in our well-being, you will embark on an AWE (Awe, Wonder, and Exploration) intervention—an intentional curation of activities and experiences designed to inspire and invigorate you, building upon the concepts explored in Chapter 7. You will also craft custom "Vibe Lists," leveraging the transformative power of music to set your mood and energy. And you will establish your virtual bookshelf, embracing the therapeutic and enlightening power of books to support your well-being and continued learning.

Finally, recognizing that personal growth is an ongoing journey, you will create a celebratory milestone tracker. This tool will help you acknowledge and honor small wins, document key learnings from setbacks, and commemorate major milestones along the way. By celebrating progress—no matter how incremental—you cultivate motivation, resilience, and a deepened sense of fulfillment in your pursuit of a purpose-driven life.

You have already taken a bold step by engaging with this work, challenging old narratives, and opening yourself to new perspectives. Trust yourself. Honor your progress. And most importantly, embrace the dynamic, ever-unfolding journey ahead with an open heart and mind.

The best version of yourself is not a fixed destination—it is a lifelong process of evolution. And you, just as you are in this moment, are already enough; now we are adding the layers and the icing.

Appendix: Actionable Worksheets

Self-Discovery Worksheet

In this exercise we will lay the foundation for self-exploration. This work will help set the stage for applying all you have explored in this book and for the interactive worksheets to follow.

As you answer each reflective question, give yourself the time and space to explore your thoughts fully. Approach this process with curiosity and grace, and reflect without judgment. There are no right or wrong answers—only honest insights! The more open you are, the more valuable this journey of self-discovery will be.

Section One: Self-Esteem and Confidence

Prompt One: What are the assets you love about yourself most?

____

____

____

Prompt Two: What do others often compliment you on?

____

____

____

Prompt Three: When do you feel most confident?

____

____

____

Section Two: Your Growth Mindset

Prompt One: What past challenges have you overcome that made you stronger?

____

____

____

Prompt Two: How do you handle fear and doubt?

____

____

____

Prompt Three: How do you react when you make mistakes?

____

____

____

Section Three: Purpose and Passion

Prompt One: What activities make you feel most alive?

____

____

____

Prompt Two: What topics do you love talking about for hours?

___

___

___

Prompt Three: If money was not a factor, how would you spend your days?

___

___

___

Section Four: Relationships

Prompt One: What kind of people do you naturally gravitate toward?

___

___

___

Prompt Two: Do your relationships support or drain you?

___

___

___

Prompt Three, Part One: For relationships that fuel you, how do you show support back?

___

___

___

Prompt Three, Part Two: For relationships that drain you, what boundaries do you struggle to enforce?

___

___

___

Section Five: Self-Compassion and Emotional Wellness

Prompt One: How do you celebrate yourself?

____

____

____

Prompt Two: What self-care rituals make you feel most restored?

____

____

____

Prompt Three: How do you show yourself compassion when you're struggling?

____

____

____

Section Six: Looking Back and Looking Forward

Prompt One: If your younger self could see you now, what would they say?

____

____

____

Prompt Two: What's one piece of advice your future self would give you?

____

____

____

Affirmation Card Set: Quarter One

TIME TO ELEVATE your mindset, with quarterly positivity. In each box, save your "*I am, I choose to*" mantra for you to reference daily to inspire and support the goals you set to achieve.

End of Exercise Prompt

At the end of the quarter check back with your hand of cards. How did your affirmations serve you? Did you follow through with your aspirations? If not, what will that inform for the next quarter and set of cards.

I am. . .

-The Purpose Pivot-

Mirror, Mirror on the Wall Card Set: Quarter One

BUILDING UPON YOUR affirmation card deck, this will stimulate your "Mirror, Mirror on the Wall: I WILL" statements. Recall Chapter 4—solidifying the things you will put on your important list: Write it, read it, say it to yourself, say it out loud. These are the phrases you can say to yourself throughout the week to will your vision into reality.

I WILL

-The Purpose Pivot-

Affirmation Card Set: Quarter Two

CONTINUE YOUR SECOND quarter of quarterly positivity. This time, in each box, save your "I am, I love. . ." mantra for you to reference daily to inspire and support the goals you set to achieve.

At the end of the quarter, check back with your hand of cards. How did your affirmations serve you? Did you follow through with your aspirations? If not, what will that inform for the next quarter and set of cards?

I give myself permission to. . .

-The Purpose Pivot-

I am. . .

-The Purpose Pivot-

I give myself permission to. . .

-The Purpose Pivot-

Mirror, Mirror on the Wall: Quarter Two

Building upon your affirmation card deck, this will stimulate your "Mirror, Mirror on the Wall: I WILL" statements. Recall Chapter 4—solidifying the things you will put on your important list: Write it, read it, say it to yourself, say it out loud. These are the phrases you can say to yourself throughout the week to will your vision into reality.

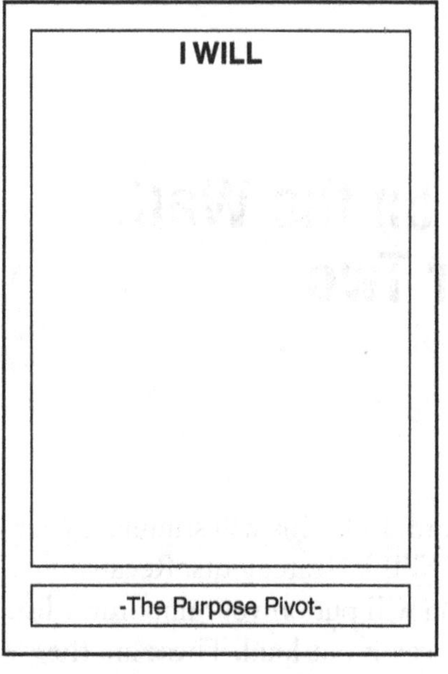

I WILL

-The Purpose Pivot-

Affirmation Card Set: Quarter Three

Continue your third quarter of quarterly positivity. This time in each box, save your "*I am, I grow when*" mantra for you to reference daily to inspire and support the goals you set to achieve.

At the end of the quarter check back with your hand of cards. How did your affirmations serve you? Did you follow through with your aspirations? If not, what will that inform for the next quarter and set of cards?

I am. . .

-The Purpose Pivot-

Mirror, Mirror on the Wall: Quarter Three

BUILDING UPON YOUR affirmation card deck, this will stimulate your "Mirror, Mirror on the Wall: I WILL" statements. Recall Chapter 4—solidifying the things you will put on your important list: Write it, read it, say it to yourself, say it out loud. These are the phrases you can say to yourself throughout the week to will your vision into reality.

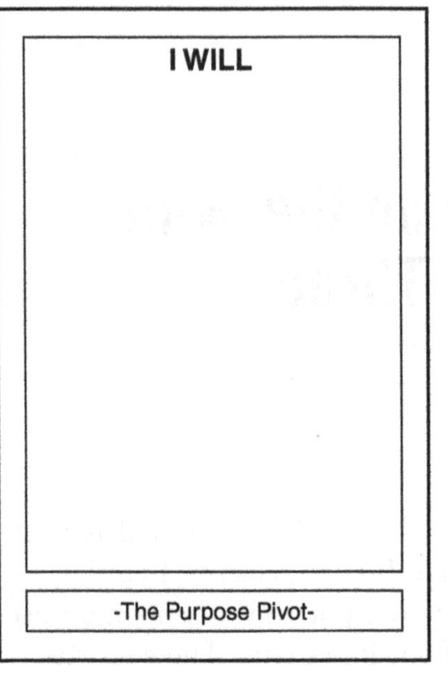
I WILL
-The Purpose Pivot-

I WILL
-The Purpose Pivot-

I WILL
-The Purpose Pivot-

I WILL
-The Purpose Pivot-

Affirmation Card Set: Quarter Four

CONTINUE YOUR FOURTH quarter of quarterly positivity. This time in each box, follow the four unique prompts to inspire the mantra for you to reference daily to support the goals you set to achieve.

At the end of the quarter/year, check back with your hand of cards. How did your affirmations serve you? Did you follow through with your aspirations? How did your relationship with your affirmations evolve throughout the year?

I am. . .

-The Purpose Pivot-

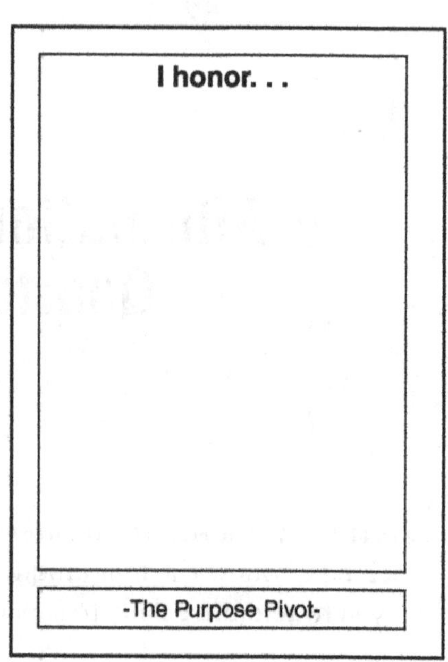

I give myself permission to shed. . .

-The Purpose Pivot-

Mirror, Mirror on the Wall: Quarter Four

BUILDING UPON YOUR affirmation card deck, this will stimulate your "Mirror, Mirror on the Wall: I WILL" statements. Recall Chapter 4—solidifying the things you will put on your important list: Write it, read it, say it to yourself, say it out loud. These are the phrases you can say to yourself throughout the week to will your vision into reality.

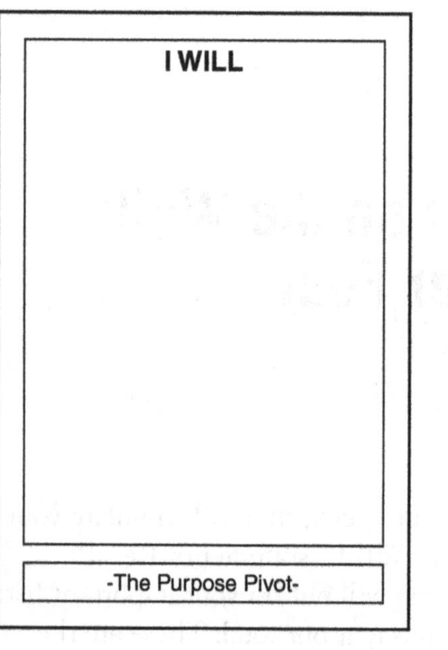
I WILL
-The Purpose Pivot-

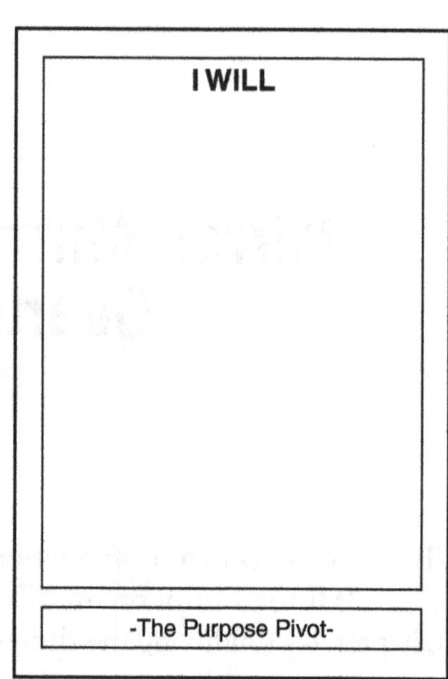
I WILL
-The Purpose Pivot-

I WILL
-The Purpose Pivot-

I WILL
-The Purpose Pivot-

Delegation List

DELEGATION IS AN effective and powerful form of self-care and supports us on our leadership paths.

AS ILLUSTRATED THROUGH numerous stories throughout the book, whether it's in your personal or professional life, making space by delegation allows us to step into our higher selves and focus on the things that matter most.

IN THIS EXERCISE, let's start to map out two lists: *things no one can do but you, things you can delegate to others*

Exercise One: Populate Your Two-Column Delegation Table

As you work through this section, here are some dynamics to keep in mind:

Things no one can do but you: emotional self-care, things of high importance

Things you can delegate: repetitive routine tasks, things of supportive importance

Now, ask yourself:

Is this something only I can do? If YES, keep it; If NO, delegate it

Is this something of high-impact? If YES, keep it; If NO, delegate it

Things No One Can Do But You	Things You Can Delegate
Ex: Creating Content	Collating Files

Exercise Two: Your Energy & Fulfillment Table

Now, ask yourself:

Is this something I enjoy doing? If YES, keep it; If NO, delegate it

Energizes Me	Depletes Me	Can Be Delegated (Yes or No)
		YES

Reflection Prompts:

Prompt One: What is stopping you from delegating? Is it a place of fear and trust or necessity?

Prompt Two: How will delegating help you grow and evolve?

Prompt Three: What will you gain by letting go?

My Awe Intervention List

An *Awe Intervention* list is a curated set of activities or experiences designed to elicit feelings of awe—a powerful emotional response that occurs when we encounter something vast, beautiful, and enhancing to our mental state. Reflecting on Chapter 7, here we will create your awe moments cheat sheet, with dedicated categories to inspire you:

Post-List Prompt One: Once you have filled in your lists, ask yourself which are awe moments you can bring into your daily or weekly routines and which ones are more "Awe Bucket List" items.

Post-List Prompt Two: For Bucket List items, set goals to achieve, even if once a year.

Nature-Based Awe:

1. EX: Watching the Sunrise
2. ____________________
3. ____________________
4. ____________________
5. ____________________

Why Nature: Connection to nature helps reduce stress levels and foster connection with self.

Creativity-Based Awe:

1. EX: Listening to an acapella group
2. ____________________
3. ____________________
4. ____________________
5. ____________________

Why Creativity: Connection to arts, music, poetry, and film is known to stimulate brain activity.

Travel and Culturally Based Awe:

1. EX: Visiting the top of the Eiffel Tower
2. ____________________
3. ____________________
4. ____________________
5. ____________________

Why Travel and Culture: Travel provides a sense of novelty and intellectual expansion.

Acts of Kindness–Based Awe:

1. EX: Volunteering at an animal shelter
2. ____________________
3. ____________________
4. ____________________
5. ____________________

Why Acts of Kindness: A shift to help others enhances gratitude and reshifts one's perspective.

Awe Moment Journal Entries

As you experience your awe moments, make space for personal reflections and processing, allowing yourself to explore the power these moments and experiences can have on your Purpose Pivot journey.

Journal Entry One

What awe-inspiring experience did you have?

____

Is this a daily, weekly, or rare occurrence? _________________________

How did this moment make you feel physically and emotionally?

____

Did this experience shift your energy? In what way?

____

How can you intentionally incorporate this kind of awe into your daily life?

____

Journal Entry Two

What awe-inspiring experience did you have?

____

Is this a daily, weekly, or rare occurrence? _________________________

How did this moment make you feel physically and emotionally?

____

Did this experience shift your energy? In what way?

____

How can you intentionally incorporate this kind of awe into your daily life?

____

My Vibe(s) List

MUSIC HAS A *transformative mood- and energy-setting power*. It can evoke emotions, it can uplift, and it can be your companion when you need to sing, dance, or cry your heart out. Reflecting on Chapters 5 and 7, here you will be your own vibe director. Create four moods you want to evoke, starting with the first pre-set prompt, and create an associated playlist of songs you can then program on your music app of choice.

Prompt 1: Notice the energy shift. Does it make you more present? Does it unlock ideas?

Prompt 2: Does the music inspire any mental imagery or visual scenes? What do you see?

VIBE: "My Pump Me Up" List

1. ____________________
2. ____________________
3. ____________________
4. ____________________
5. ____________________
6. ____________________
7. ____________________
8. ____________________
9. ____________________
10. ____________________

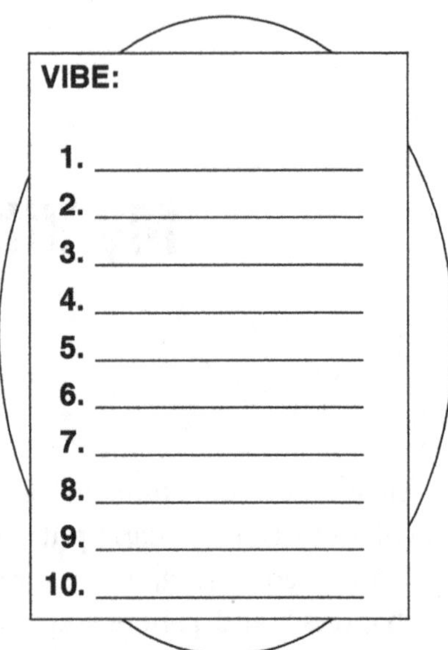

VIBE:

1. ____________________
2. ____________________
3. ____________________
4. ____________________
5. ____________________
6. ____________________
7. ____________________
8. ____________________
9. ____________________
10. ____________________

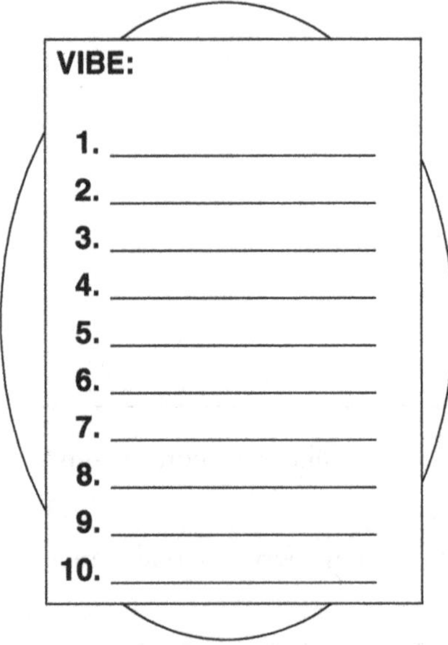

VIBE:

1. ____________________
2. ____________________
3. ____________________
4. ____________________
5. ____________________
6. ____________________
7. ____________________
8. ____________________
9. ____________________
10. ____________________

VIBE:

1. ____________________
2. ____________________
3. ____________________
4. ____________________
5. ____________________
6. ____________________
7. ____________________
8. ____________________
9. ____________________
10. ____________________

Bibliotherapy

Bibliotherapy is the therapeutic use of books and reading to support mental health and well-being. It can be used for personal growth, emotional healing, and stress relief. This worksheet will serve as your personal Bookshelf Reference:

As you read new books explore:

Prompt One: Identify themes or issues you want to explore: What are some challenges you're currently facing? What are some topics you're curious about or want to learn more about? What do you feel you need more of? Inspiration / Laughter / Perspective / Coping Strategies / Self-Discovery / Other: ___________

Prompt Two: Set Reading Goals and Intentions: How many books do you want to read per month? What do you hope to gain from this reading experience?

Self-awareness / Coping Skills / Emotional Release / Inspiration / Entertainment / Other: ___________

Prompt Three: Reflect on Your Readings or Rereadings. Did any part of the story or message resonate with you? Why? How can you apply the insights gained in your daily life?

This Bookshelf Belongs To: ______________________

Books I Have Read:	**Books Recommended to Me:**
Personal Self-Discovery and Growth	**Self-Discovery and Growth**
1. ______	1. ______
2. ______	2. ______
Key Learnings: ______ ______	
Emotional Healing and Mental Wellness	**Emotional Healing and Mental Wellness**
1. ______	1. ______
2. ______	2. ______
Key Learnings: ______ ______	
Inspirational/Motivational/ Spiritual	**Inspirational/Motivational**
1. ______	1. ______
2. ______	2. ______
Key Learnings: ______ ______	**Mindfulness/Spirituality**
	1. ______
	2. ______

Self-Discovery and Growth: *(Books that encourage introspection, self-awareness, and personal evolution)*
Emotional Healing and Mental Wellness: *(Books that provide tools for processing emotions, managing mental health, and healing past wounds)*
Inspirational/Motivational: *(Books to inspire action, resilience, and courage in the face of challenges)*
Mindfulness/Spirituality: *(Books that guide mindfulness practices, inner peace, and spiritual exploration)*

Milestone Tracker Worksheet

Reflecting on Chapter 5, as we grow, we must show ourselves grace—from acknowledging the small wins along the way, to learning from setbacks, to celebrating the major milestones. In this worksheet, we will celebrate the progress we often overlook and make achievements more tangible.

Milestone Tracker: Goal One

For my first goal, I will:

____

What do two wins along your journey look like:

Small Win: ______________________________

Nearing Goal Win: ________________________

Start Date and Goal Date: ________________________

Dive into 3 sections:
1/3 of the way/Small Win date:
2/3 of the way/Learning Point date:
3/3 Victory!

Small Win (date and journal entry):

____

Learning Point (date and journal entry):

____

Victory! (date and journal entry):

____

What is your celebration plan?

____

Milestone Tracker: Goal Two

For my second goal, I will:

____

What do two wins along your journey look like:

Small Win: ______________________________

Nearing Goal Win: __________________________

Start Date and Goal Date: ________________________

Dive into 3 sections:
1/3 of the way/Small Win date:
2/3 of the way/Learning Point date:
3/3 Victory!

Small Win (date and journal entry):

____

Learning Point (date and journal entry):

____

Victory! (date and journal entry):

____

What is your celebration plan?

____

Milestone Tracker: Goal Three

For my third goal, I will:

____

What do two wins along your journey look like:

Small Win: ___________________________________

Nearing Goal Win: ______________________________

Start Date and Goal Date: ___________________________

Dive into 3 sections:

1/3 of the way/Small Win date:
2/3 of the way/Learning Point date:
3/3 Victory!

Small Win (date and journal entry):

____

Learning Point (date and journal entry):

____

Victory! (date and journal entry):

____

What is your celebration plan?

____

Notes

Chapter 1

1. Kahneman, D. (2011). *Thinking, Fast and Slow*. Farrar, Straus and Giroux.
2. Pigliucci, M. (2012). *Answers for Aristotle: How Science and Philosophy Can Lead Us to a More Meaningful Life*. Basic Books.
3. Gladwell, M. (2005). *Blink: The Power of Thinking Without Thinking*. Back Bay Books.
4. James, W. *Principles of Psychology*. Wikipedia.
5. Goleman, D. (1995). *Emotional Intelligence: Why It Can Matter More Than IQ*. Bantam.
6. Andrews S. (2021). "Are Men and Women Equally Emotionally Intelligent?" https://www.drshawnandrews.com/blogs/are-men-and-women-equally-emotionally-intelligent.
7. Damasio, A.R. (1994). *Descartes' Error: Emotion, Reason, and the Human Brain*. Putnam.
8. Headspace.com. Meditations and Quotes.
9. American Lung Association. Lung Capacity & Aging.
10. Maidique, M.A. (2011). "Decoding Intuition for More Effective Decision-Making." *Harvard Business Review*.
11. Berger, Nancy. LinkedIn Post. https://www.linkedin.com/posts/nancy-berger-a6105817_career-goals-gratitude-activity-7031984878720053248-yddt.

Chapter 2

1. Aligned Modern Health. A Functional Medicine Guide to Adrenal Fatigue, May 16, 2021.
2. Baik, J.H. (2020). Stress and the dopaminergic reward system. *Experimental & Molecular Medicine* 52: 1879–1890.
3. Broitt, T.W., Adler, A.B., and Bartone, P.T. (2001). Deriving benefits from stressful events: the role of engagement in meaningful work and hardiness. *Journal of Occupational Health Psychology* 6 (1): 53–63.
4. Scheier, M.F. and Carver, C.S. (1993). On the power of positive thinking: The benefits of being optimistic. *Current Directions in Psychological Science* 2 (1): 26–30.
5. McGregor, B.A., Antoni, M.H., et al. (2004). Cognitive–behavioral stress management increases benefit finding and immune function among women with early-stage breast cancer. *J Psychosom Res*. 56 (1): 1–8.
6. Bower, J.E., Moskowitz, J.T., and Epel, E. (2009). Pathways linking positive life changes after stress and physical health outcomes. *Current Directions in Psychological Science* 18: 337–341.
7. Selye, H. (1973). The evolution of the stress concept. *American Scientist* 61: 692–699.
8. Steiner-Hofbauer, V. and Holzinger, A. (2020). *How to cope with the challenges of medical education? Stress, depression, and coping in undergraduate medical students*. *Acad Psychiatry* 44 (4): 380–387.
9. Mayo Clinic. Stress symptoms: Effects on your body and behavior.
10. Mayo Clinic. Stress symptoms: Effects on your body and behavior.
11. Cleveland Clinic. Adrenal Crisis. https://my.clevelandclinic.org/health/diseases/23948-adrenal-crisis.
12. Harvard Business Review. (2024). Dopamine: The pathway to pleasure (https://www.health.harvard.edu/mind-and-mood/dopamine-the-pathway-to-pleasure).
13. Harvard Business Review. (2024). Dopamine: The pathway to pleasure (https://www.health.harvard.edu/mind-and-mood/dopamine-the-pathway-to-pleasure).
14. Domschke, K. and Gottschalk, M.G. (2019). Genetics of Anxiety and Stress-Related Disorders—Toward a Bottom-up Cross-Disorder Psychopathology. *JAMA Psychiatry* 76 (9): 889–890.
15. MentalHealth.com, 2024. The Long-Term Consequences of Negative Stress.
16. Dr. Judith Gurdian, Capital Women's Care, Rockville, Maryland.

17. Annual Reviews, Estrogen, Stress, and Depression: Cognitive and Biological Interactions (https://www.annualreviews.org/content/journals/10.1146/annurev-clinpsy-050718-095557).
18. Dr. Judith A Gurdian, Capital Women's Care, Rockville, Maryland, "The Connection Between Stress & Your Hormones."
19. John Hopkins Medical, Women's Health.
20. Schmidt, P.J. et al. (2015). Hormones and mood: The role of estrogen and progesterone. *Journal of Clinical Psychiatry*.
21. Dr. Jessica Shepard. (2024). *Generation M: Living Well in Perimenopause and Menopause*.
22. Masterclass (2024). *The Magic of Menopause*, Halle Berry, Dr. Judith Joseph, Dr. Emily Jacobs, Dr. Lori Brotto, Dr. Jen Gutner.
23. Fadel, Tamsen. (2024). *The M Factor: Shredding the Silence on Menopause, documentary, PBS*.
24. Kelley, G.A., Kelley, K.S., and Pate, R.R. (2017). Effect of resistance exercise on body mass index, body composition, and metabolic rate in adults: A systematic review and meta-analysis. *European Journal of Sport Science*.
25. Kelley, G.A., Kelley, K.S., and Pate, R.R. (2017). Effect of resistance exercise on body mass index, body composition, and metabolic rate in adults: A systematic review and meta-analysis. *European Journal of Sport Science*.
26. Tanner, E.M., Jones, C.D., and Esser, K.A. (2021). The impact of resistance exercise on neuromuscular function and performance in aging. *Journal of Gerontology: Medical Sciences*.
27. Masterclass (2024). Gut Health with David Zilber, Dr. Emeran Mayer, Erica Sonnenburg, and Justin Sonnenburg.
28. Calder, P.C. (2020). Omega-3 fatty acids and inflammation. *Nutrients* 12 (7): 2084.
29. Dawson, R.G., et al. (2014). Vitamin C and immune function: An overview of the effects on gut health. *Nutrients*.
30. Bailey, C.H. (2015). Synaptic plasticity and memory: An evaluation of the hypothesis. *Neurobiology of Learning and Memory*.
31. Calder, P.C. (2020). Omega-3 fatty acids and inflammation. *Nutrients* 12 (7): 2084.
32. Laukkanen, T., & Laukkanen, J. A. (2016). Sauna bathing improves cardiovascular health. *Progress in Cardiovascular Diseases*.
33. Shevchuk, N.A. (2008). Adapted cold shower as a potential treatment for depression. *Medical Hypotheses* 70 (5): 995–1001.
34. Brody, S. (2010). The relative health benefits of different sexual activities. *Journal of Sexual Medicine* 7 (4): 1336–1361.

Chapter 3

1. Cormier, D. L., & Ataabadi, Y.A. (2022). Self-compassion and self-criticism in response to societal feedback. National Institutes of Health.
2. Mills, J.S. and Samson, L. (2022). Body image shame and self-criticism in adulthood. *Frontiers in Psychology*.
3. Jones, S.M. (2021). Cultivating Self-Compassion in Cognitive Behavioral Therapy, Challenging your self-critical thoughts. *Psychology Today*.
4. Jones, S.M. (2021). Cultivating Self-Compassion in Cognitive Behavioral Therapy, Challenging your self-critical thoughts. *Psychology Today*.
5. Kirby, Elle. Understanding and Overcoming Negative Body Image. Balanced Awakening (https://balancedawakening.com/blog/understanding-and-overcoming-negative-body-image).
6. Lebsack, Lexy. (2024). Beauty & Wellness Briefing: What's next for the rapidly-growing scar-care category? (https://www.glossy.co/beauty/wellness/beauty-wellness-briefing-whats-next-for-the-rapidly-growing-scar-care-category/).
7. Mills, J.S. and Samson, L. (2022). Body image shame and self-criticism in adulthood. *Frontiers in Psychology*.
8. Gurian, M. (2013). *The Wonder of Aging: A New Approach to Embracing Life After Fifty*. Atria Books.

Chapter 4

1. Maslow, A.H., (1943). A theory of human motivation. *Psychological Review* 50(4): 370–396.
2. Kaufman, S.B. (2020). *Transcend: The New Science of Self-Actualization*. TarcherPerigee.
3. Brown, B. (2012). *Daring Greatly: How the Courage to Be Vulnerable Transforms the Way We Live, Love, Parent, and Lead.* Avery.
4. Dweck, C.S. (2006). Mindset: The New Psychology of Success: How we can learn to fulfill our potential.
5. Maslow, A.H. (1943). A theory of human motivation. *Psychological Review* 50(4): 370–396.
6. Mel Robbins. 2024: How to Manifest Anything You Want & Unlock the Unlimited Power of Your Mind. Podcast.
7. Doty, J. (2024). Mind Magic: The Neuroscience of Manifestation & How It Changes Everything.
8. Hebb, D.O, (1949). *The Organization of Behavior, A Neuropsychological Theory*. Wiley.

9. Mel Robbins. (2024). How to Manifest Anything You Want & Unlock the Unlimited Power of Your Mind. Podcast.
10. Shams, L., & Seitz, A.R. (2008). Benefits of multisensory learning. *Trends in Cognitive Sciences* 12(11): 411–417.
11. Neff, K. (2011). *Self-Compassion: The Proven Power of Being Kind to Yourself.* HarperCollins.
12. Build with Leila Hormozi Podcast. (2024). Freedom Isn't the Ability to Say Yes.
13. Abramson, Ashley. (2021). The Ethical Imperative of Self Care. American Psychology Association.

Chapter 5

1. Rogers, C.R., (1961). *On Becoming a Person: A Therapist's View of Psychotherapy*. Houghton Mifflin Harcourt.
2. John Hopkins, https://www.hopkinsmedicine.org/health/conditions-and-diseases/uterine-fibroids.
3. Rogers, C.R., (1961). *On Becoming a Person: A Therapist's View of Psychotherapy*. Houghton Mifflin Harcourt.
4. Kitayama, Shinobu. (2017). "Attitudes and social cognition." *Journal of Personality and Social Psychology* 112 (34): 357–360.
5. Neff, K., 2011: *Self-Compassion: The Proven Power of Being Kind to Yourself.* William Morrow.
6. Fiat, A., Herbst, R.B., Behm, K., Turner, B., & Cross, J. (2024). Spiritual practices and trauma healing. *Clinical Practice in Psychology*.
7. Miller, Lisa. 2024: *The Awakened Brain, The New Science of Spirituality and Our Quest for an Inspired Life*. Random House.
8. Tolle, Eckhart. 2024: *The Power of Now: A Guide to Spiritual Enlightenment.* New World Library.

Chapter 6

1. Hoey, Kelly. (2017). *Build Your Dream Network*, Penguin Random House.
2. Godman, Heidi. (April 2023). *Can Varied Social Interactions Boost Well-Being*. Harvard Health Publishing.
3. Hostinar, Camelia E., & Gunnar, Megan R. (2016). *Social Support Can Buffer against Stress and Shape Brain Activity*. National Library of Medicine.
4. Holt-Lunstad, Julianne, Smith, Timothy B., & Bradley, Layton J. (July 2010). Social Relationships and Mortality Risk: A Meta-Analytic Review. *PLOS Medicine*.

5. Tan, Qin, et al. (2023). Effectiveness of Peer Support on Quality of Life and Anxiety in Breast Cancer Patients: A Systematic Review and Meta-Analysis. *Breast Care (Basel)* 18(1): 49–59.
6. Tang, Y.-Y., Hölzel, Britta K., & Posner, Michael I. (2015). The neuroscience of mindfulness meditation. *Nature Reviews Neuroscience* 16(4): 213–225.
7. Csikszentmihalyi, M., (2008). *Flow: The Psychology of Optimal Experience*. Harper Perennial Modern Classics.
8. Griffiths et al., (2018). Psychedelic-Assisted Psychotherapy: A Systematic Review of Context, Design, and Methodology.
9. Uchino, Bert. (2004). *Social Support and Physical Health: Understanding the Health Consequences of Relationships*. Yale University Press.

Chapter 7

1. Pabon, R.J., Agravante, J., Ignacio, C., & Susaya, L.M. (January 2025). A Qualitative Study on Millennials' Experiences of FOMO and JOMO. ResearchGate.net.
2. Rautela, S., & Sharma, S. (2022). Fear of missing out (FOMO) to the joy of missing out (JOMO): Shifting dunes of problematic usage of the internet among social media users. *Journal of Information, Communication and Ethics in Society* 20(4): 461–479.
3. Eitan, T., & Gazit, T. (2023). No social media for six hours? The emotional experience of Meta's global outage according to FoMO, JoMO and Internet Intensity. *ScienceDirect*.
4. Vasovagal Syncope, Cleveland Clinic. (June 2022).
5. Raichle, M.E. (2015). The Brain's Default Mode Network. *Annual Review of Neuroscience* 38: 433–447.
6. Walsh, Jennifer, & Olsen, Monica. (2024). *Biophilic Solutions* podcast, multiple episodes.
7. Walsh, Jennifer. (2022). Walk Your Way Calm. *Prevention* magazine.
8. American Lung Association, May 2021.
9. Yadav, Upasana, & Pandey, Neerja. (September 2024). Body Humors, Personality Traits and Emotional Regulation in Adolescents. *International Journal of Research and Analytical Reviews* 11(3): 711–718.
10. Keltner, D., & Haidt, J. (2003). Approaching awe, a moral, spiritual, and aesthetic emotion. *Cognition & Emotion* 17(2): 297–314.
11. Backus, Massimo. (2024). *Human First, Leader Second: How Self-Compassion Outperforms Self-Criticism*. Berrett-Koehler Publishers.

Chapter 8

1. Bremner, J.D. (2005). Effects of traumatic stress on brain structure and function: Relevance to early responses to trauma. *Journal of Trauma & Dissociation* 6, 51–68. Taylor & Francis.
2. Bremner, J.D., & Elzinga, B. (2007). Structural and functional plasticity of the human brain in posttraumatic stress disorder. *ScienceDirect*.
3. Oren, E., Gündoğmuş, I., & Yaser, A.B. (2024). EMDR and the AIP model: Healing the scars of trauma. *Frontiers in Psychiatry* 15: 1469787.
4. Bremner, J.D., & Elzinga, B. (2007). Structural and functional plasticity of the human brain in posttraumatic stress disorder. *ScienceDirect*.
5. B.L. Fredrickson. (2001). The role of positive emotions in positive psychology: The broaden-and-build theory of positive emotions. National Library of Medicine.
6. Oren, E., Gündoğmuş, I., & Yaser, A.B. (2024). EMDR and the AIP model: Healing the scars of trauma. *Frontiers in Psychiatry* 15: 1469787.
7. Neff, K.D. (2012). The science of self-compassion, In C. Germer & R. Siegel (Eds.), *Compassion and Wisdom in Psychotherapy* (pp. 79–92). Guilford Press.
8. Ramtin, S., Ngoue, M., Ring, D., & Teunis, T. (2024). The central sensitization inventory measures thoughts and emotions, *SAGE Journals*. 10.1177/23743735241273589.
9. Barillas, Trish. (2024).A Mindfulness Approach to Anxiety Management. TrishBarillas.com.
10. Kashdan, T.B., & Rottenberg, J. (2010). Psychological flexibility as a fundamental aspect of health. *Clinical Psychology Review* 30(7): 865–878.
11. Biedermann, H. (1992). *Dictionary of Symbolism: Cultural Icons and the Meanings Behind Them*. Oxford University Press.

Chapter 9

1. Baird, B., Smallwood, J., Mrazek, M. D., Kam, J. W., Franklin, M. S., & Schooler, J. W. (2012). Inspired by distraction: mind wandering facilitates creative incubation. *Psychological Science* 23(10): 1117–1122.
2. Sloan, Denise. (2025). International Society for Traumatic Stress Studies, *Journal of Traumatic Stress*. Wiley Publishing.
3. American Psychological Association, APA *Dictionary of Psychology*, updated November 15, 2023.
4. Dabrowski, Kazimierz. (2015). *Personality-Shaping Through Positive Disintegration*. Red Pill Press.
5. Davis, Tchiki. (2015). *Personal Growth: Definition, Goals, & Examples*. Berkley Well-Being Institute. https://www.berkeleywellbeing.com/personal-growth.html.

Acknowledgments

ANY PROJECT OF impact is made possible by the support, expertise, and generosity of remarkable individuals. I am deeply grateful to those who have contributed their time, knowledge, and encouragement throughout this journey. Their belief in my vision has been both inspiring and instrumental in bringing it to life.

From my husband and daughter, who supported me as I wrote every weekend for months on end, to my family and friends who not only contributed to this book but also opened their own networks with generous introductions to support the success of my research endeavors—your support has meant everything. To my family, who cheered me on from the moment I shared my vision and my partnership with Wiley Publishing, and to my friends—published book authors, journalists, and ghostwriters—who volunteered to mentor me with invaluable advice on how to get the most out of my interviews, I am beyond grateful.

To the amazing women of DealMakeHers, who opened doors for me throughout this entire process with introductions and references, and to each woman who sat with me to share their incredible stories—you have not only made an impact on me but on the process as a whole, expanding my perspective and uncovering new opportunities.

To the women specifically who joined me on Zoom calls, in-person interviews, text conversations, and more and whose contribution, collaboration, and passion have played a pivotal role in this work: Atoya Burleson, Tai Beauchamp, Nancy Berger, Trish Barillas, Kendra Bracken-Ferguson, Stacy Berns, Sheena Butler-Young, Dr. Patricia David, Antonia Saint Dunbar, Khirma Eliazov, Alicia Esposito, Mina Fader, Emma Grede, Keri Glassman, Jennifer Gootman, Mindy Grossman, Melissa Guerrero, Modupé Whyelaé Rouse, Jane Hanson, Kelly Hoey, Nicole Leinbach Hoffman, Stacy Igel, Sarah Kugelman Jill Katz, Alice Kim, Lolita Lopez, Cate Luzio, Lisa Mateo, Chiara Mecozzi, Rebecca Minkoff, Sally Mueller, Joelle Oliver, Maryln Ortiz, Kristen Paladino, Clarissa Ramos-Cafarelli, Shirley Ramos Roseman, Kristy Rotonde, Jamie Schofield Riva, Amy Shecter, Alexis Thomas, Yvette Vargas, and Stacey Widlitz.

A special appreciation also goes to Dr. Somi Javaid and Dr. Kavitha Persaud for their invaluable medical insights, and to Meg Hainer ob-gyn, whose expertise and dedication have been instrumental to me on many personal levels.

And finally, to every person who has come to me with ideas on how to amplify the reach of this work so that we can impact as many readers as possible—thank you. Your contributions have enriched this journey in ways words cannot fully express. This reach of this endeavor would not be possible without you.

About the Author

Melissa Gonzalez is a visionary in understanding brand positioning through the study of behaviors and insights. As a principal at MG2 and shareholder at Colliers Engineering and Design, she drives innovative strategies that help brands create meaningful connections through immersive storytelling and future-forward design.

Melissa's journey began on Wall Street, where she honed her analytical and business acumen in institutional equity sales. Drawn to the evolving dynamics of brands, she pivoted from finance to retail, founding The Lionesque Group in 2012. Her firm quickly became a leader in pop-up retail, launching over 150 consumer experiences for startups and Fortune 500 companies alike. Recognized as a pioneer in the "pop-up revolution," she authored *The Pop-Up Paradigm: How Brands Build Human Connections in a Digital Age*, solidifying her expertise in omnichannel retail and consumer experiences.

In 2020, The Lionesque Group was acquired by MG2, now part of Colliers Engineering and Design, where Melissa continues to push the boundaries of experiential design. That same year, she launched Retail Refined, a podcast exploring the future of retail and consumer experiences and the key forces shaping industry disruption. A sought-after speaker, she has graced the stages of SXSW, Shoptalk, World

Retail Congress, NRF's Retail's Big Show, and Vogue Business Summit. In the media, you may have seen her ringing NASDAQ's opening bell or in the *New York Times*.

Beyond her professional impact, Melissa is celebrated for her genuine curiosity and commitment to helping others succeed. She is a passionate mentor, championing women in leadership, and consistently emphasizes the power of fostering impactful communities. Now she takes her advocacy further with her latest book, *The Purpose Pivot: How Dynamic Leaders Put Vulnerability and Intuition into Action*, offering a bold framework for leadership in an ever-evolving world.

Index